BEHIND BARS

BEHIND BARS

Prisons in America

Edited by Richard Kwartler

Vintage Books • A Division of Random House • New York

VINTAGE BOOKS EDITION, JUNE 1977
First Edition
Copyright © 1974, 1975, 1976, 1977 by
Correctional Information Service, Inc.
All rights reserved under International and
Pan-American Copyright Conventions.
Published in the United States by Random House, Inc.,
New York, and simultaneously in
Canada by Random House of Canada Limited, Toronto.

Library of Congress Cataloging in Publication Data
Main entry under title:

Behind bars.

Reprinted from Corrections magazine, Sept. 1974–June 1976.
1. Corrections—United States. 2. Prisons—United States.
3. Community-based corrections—United States.
I. Kwartler, Richard. II. Corrections magazine.
HV9304.B43   365′.973   76–62495
ISBN 0–394–72196–9

Manufactured in the United States of America

Cover photo by Bill Powers for *Corrections Magazine*.

Acknowledgments

This book is based primarily on material from *Corrections Magazine,* the first publication devoted exclusively to original reporting on prison systems in all fifty states. Michael S. Serrill and Steve Gettinger are the authors of a major portion of the original work and also contributed additional material.

Edgar May, Anthony Astrachan and R.V. and Tia Denenberg are the authors of articles from which other key segments of the book are drawn.

Material from the work of Ronald H. Bailey, William E. Cockerham and Michael Kiernan is also included.

Sheila Kwartler provided valuable assistance in the editing and deserves special thanks.

Special recognition must go to Mike Sviridoff and Bob Goldmann of the Ford Foundation. Without their faith in the value of the printed word, the magazine would never have been launched.

The original material appeared in *Corrections Magazine* between September 1974 and June 1976.

Contents

Introduction

The arithmetic of crime, like the multiplication tables, has become a permanent part of American life.

There were, says the FBI, about 11.3 million serious crimes reported in 1975, up 10 percent over the year before. A breakdown shows 21 such crimes committed each minute. Only 21 percent were solved by arrests. Crime rose more in suburban and rural areas than in big cities.

In 1960, the FBI's Uniform Crime Reports show, about 160 of every 100,000 Americans were victims of violent crimes. In 1975, it was 480 of every 100,000—a 200 percent increase.

Some researchers are concerned about the completeness of crime studies—for one thing, it is believed that millions of crimes go unreported each year. But whatever their accuracy, the surveys confirm what most people already know: crime is a serious, often a frightening problem in our society. Have you or a relative or friend been a victim of crime during the last year? Put that question to anyone and the likely answer is yes. A U.S. Census Bureau study found that 40 million people were victimized by crimes in 1974. If, for example, each victim/told only four others (relatives and/or friends) about the experience, it would mean that of the total U.S. population of 211 million in 1974, 200 million were either victims themselves or had been told about a crime that victimized someone they knew.

No wonder national polls show that for Americans, fear of crime is a key worry, sometimes ranking No. 1.

As concern over crime increases, so does the public's interest in the criminal justice system and in how it might better combat lawlessness. That system has three components—police, courts and corrections. Increasingly, the public has asked the first for stricter enforcement; the second for tougher sentences; and the third, which includes the administration of the nation's prisons and community correctional facilities, for a little bit of everything.

Says Raymond K. Procunier, former director of the California Department of Corrections, the nation's largest state prison system: "What makes the last [nine] years so unique is that this is the first time that this country has ever had a sustained interest in prisons. . . . And that's the greatest blessing since sliced bread."

During his seven years as the top prison official in California, Procunier was attacked on the left by highly vocal community activists, academics and liberal legislators who called constantly for reform. He was attacked on the right by influential law enforcement officials and conservative legislators who accused him of being too easy on criminals. What the public has sought through corrections are goals that sometimes conflict, like punishment and rehabilitation. But there is also public safety (separating criminals from society) and deterrence (maintaining a strict prison system so that members of the public will be encouraged not to commit crimes). Corrections officials have never really known which goal the public favored most. As one corrections commissioner put it:

"It gets you down. . . . You can never win. . . . You go too slow for the people who write editorials on you; you go too fast for the politicians and the people."

As public interest in the prisons reached an all-time high in this decade, the corrections field was undergoing profound change. It may never be the same.

For 150 years, the concept of rehabilitation has been a prime concern of prison systems in the United States. Following a so-called medical model, the institution viewed the offender as someone sick who could be treated, reformed and returned to society as a law-abiding citizen. But as the 70's began, the rehabilitation concept for adult inmates came under blistering attack. By 1975, it was in full retreat on some fronts.

Prisons, claim the critics of rehabilitation, can't really help anyone, and rehabilitation doesn't work. That's been demonstrated, the critics argue, by the statistics on recidivism (return to criminal activity by former inmates). Let's finally admit it, say the critics, who add: Use prisons for what they can do—punish lawbreakers who deserve it. Punishments should be fair and uniform. There should be general use of short, flat sentences, no parole, and no indeterminate sentences (like one year to life, with the parole board determining release based on an inmate's progress in being "rehabilitated").

These ideas are gaining in popularity. A few states have already adopted them. Top prison administrators are worried. In a 1975 survey conducted by *Corrections Magazine*, 63 percent of the administrators said that some rehabilitation programs could change inmate behavior for the better, and another 14 percent said there was not enough evidence to justify scrapping the rehabilitation concept.

Public disgust with high crime rates has been a factor in another major 1970's correctional phenomenon—critical overcrowding in adult prisons. More people are being sen-

Introduction

tenced to prisons, leading to these situations throughout the nation: cells designed for one inmate have three or four; inmates sleep in shower stalls, on corridor floors, and under bunks; and tents and trailers are used when cells run out.

A *Corrections Magazine* study showed that there were more adult inmates in prison on January 1, 1976, than ever before in U.S. history—250,000.

But they are only part of the corrections world. There are an additional 225,000 adult and juvenile inmates in other facilities, mainly jails and detention centers. Perhaps a million more people are on probation and parole, or are enrolled in other community programs. And federal, state and local government units spent $3.4 billion on corrections in 1974, the last full year for which figures are available. That included salaries for about 210,000 corrections personnel.

This book covers corrections in America in a new way. Rather than relying on the reports of program administrators, it uses as the basis of its coverage the exclusive on-site reporting of *Corrections Magazine.*

At the end, when all the facts have been considered, one must wonder if this statement is true: "The degree of civilization in a society can be judged by entering its prisons." Dostoevsky wrote that in 1862.

R.K.
New York, September, 1976

BEHIND BARS

Chapter 1
Inside: What It's Really Like

It was 5:30 A.M. at the Georgia State Prison at Reidsville. The seventy men in dormitory F3 struggled awake on their narrow beds. They pulled on their prison whites and shuffled, one after the other, toward the latrine at one end of the dormitory. The bathroom had no doors, no partitions, no privacy—just three toilets protruding from one wall of the room. The toilets had no seats, and the men had to sit on cold porcelain.

One of the men, when he finished, returned to his bunk. He was lean, with graying hair. He had hollow cheeks and a sunken mouth, the result of missing teeth. He was thirty-nine years old. He looked much older.

His name was Oscar Sweat. The number on his back was 64067. He was not articulate, not colorful, not angry. He was just one among 2,600 men doing time at the Reidsville prison. And he was one among the more than 475,000 men, women and children who spend their days subject to the dull routine of America's approximately 5,000 prisons, jails, juvenile training schools and detention centers.

Oscar Sweat was, in a way, luckier than most. Having

spent much of his adult life in prison, mostly for burglary and car theft, he had become accustomed to the deadening routine. The regimentation no longer bothered him—the constant waiting, and counting, and standing in line. And unlike 40 percent of Reidsville's inmates, he kept himself occupied.

Six hours a day he worked in the prison license-plate factory. In the late afternoon and early evening he and another inmate made wallets, which the prison sold for them. With this small income they had enough money to buy tobacco and other necessities. At night Sweat watched television—the high point of his day, he said. But when asked what programs he watched, he answered, "What-ever's on there."

At 11 P.M. the inmates went to bed. Lights were turned out. And on the following day Sweat went through exactly the same routine. Every day was like the last; every day was like the next.

The majority of American prison inmates live Oscar Sweat's reality. They get up in the morning, stand in line to be counted, then stand in line to eat breakfast. They go to work for a few hours, making license plates or metal furniture, shoes or street signs. Then they line up to be counted again, line up to eat lunch, and go back to work again for a few hours. Or, an increasing number do no work, because there isn't enough to go around. So they stand around the prison yard, sit idly in their cells or occupy themselves with arts and crafts. Before dinner there is an exercise period. Then they are counted again, eat a third meal and spend the evening watching television.

Occasionally there is some excitement—a fistfight, a knife fight, a riot. But for the majority who want to simply "do their bit" and get out, these incidents serve only to make their lives more uncomfortable. Such violent diver-

4

sions lead to "shakedowns" of their cells in search of weapons and other contraband, or to "lock-ups" in which all inmates are confined to their cells for days, weeks, even months at a time.

There are occasional sanctioned recreations—a movie, a performance by an outside singing group, a visit from a friend or family member. And some inmates—always a minority—spend a few hours a week taking educational and vocational courses or participating in group therapy or "self-help" activities. For an even smaller minority there are occasional visits home on "furlough," or education- and work-release. But the rule is monotonous routine, punctuated by the ringing of bells, the blaring of sirens and the clanging of steel doors and gates which mark the end of one routine activity and the beginning of another.

Of the 475,000 inmates in American correctional institutions on a given day, about 200,000 are in jails and juvenile detention centers awaiting trial or are serving jail terms of less than a year for misdemeanors. The remaining 275,000 are in state and federal prisons serving time for felony crimes. About 245,000 are adult male offenders; about 5,000 are adult women; 28,000 are juveniles. The average time served by adult men is two to three years; the women and children generally serve eighteen months or less.

Most adult male offenders are incarcerated in about 375 state and federal institutions. All but a handful of these correctional institutions are large facilities, with 500 or more inmates. Heading the list in size is the State Prison of Southern Michigan at Jackson, with 4,500 inmates. Most of the institutions are at least fifty years old, and some date back to the nineteenth century.

During the late sixties and early seventies the number of state and federal adult prisoners declined, from 220,000 in 1962 to under 200,000 for the years from 1969 through

1973. This was due principally to a vast expansion in the use of probation and other community alternatives to incarceration. Recently there has been what Harvard criminologist Lloyd Ohlin has called a "massive counterattack" by judges and parole boards against community programming. This "counterattack" has been partly responsible for sharp increases in the prison population.

In January 1976 a *Corrections Magazine* survey found that there were more adult men in prison than ever before in the history of the country. The sudden increase in prison population—25,000 in 1975 alone—has caused serious overcrowding in institutions all over the country, especially in the South. In some Southern states the prison populations had increased more than 40 percent within the previous two years; in Florida the inmate population grew as much in nine months in 1975 as it had in the previous nine years. Florida had 11,000 inmates in March 1975; it had 16,000 by the end of January 1976, and new ones were coming in at the rate of 100 a week.

By early 1976, prisoners in some states were forced to sleep on floors and in shower rooms. In Alabama, some slept on ledges above toilets. Overcrowded conditions in many U.S. prisons caused other inmates to live in unsupervised dormitories or to fit themselves by twos, threes and fours into cells built for one. While overcrowding was not a new problem, some states reported that the situation was worse than ever before. Desperate for ways to relieve this condition, administrators across the country turned for emergency housing to ships, tents, trailers, warehouses and motels. They even let some inmates go free.

Cellblock One—a five-story granite mass inside South Carolina's Central Correctional Institution—was built in 1860 to house 200 men in single cells. Over the last several years it has housed about 550. Walking gingerly along the narrow catwalk on the fifth tier of Cellblock One, a correction officer peered into a dim cell. "Ain't you overcrowded in there?" he asked for the benefit of a reporter who accompanied him. "No, sir," a voice shouted back. "We only got two in here."

Cell 16, a little farther down the catwalk, was overcrowded even by inmate standards. Like the others in Cellblock One, it was five feet wide, eight feet long and six and a half feet high. Inside were three men. Because the fifth tier held protective-custody and disciplinary cases, inmates were kept in their cells twenty-four hours a day, except for visits and weekly showers. The three inmates in Cell 16 shared two sets of clothes, two spoons and two mattresses; they had no blankets or pillows. The two older men slept on the bunks; the third, a youth with blond hair, slept in a sheet on the floor. This had been going on for two weeks, he said.

James Earl Ray, the man convicted of killing Dr. Martin Luther King, Jr., said in an interview in the Tennessee State Penitentiary, "I'd rather have a cell partner." Not long after he made that statement there were two men in all the four-and-a-half-by-eight-foot cells, and four men in the eight-by-ten-foot cells. After a riot rocked the penitentiary in September 1975, the prison kept inmates who were not on work- or education-release locked in their cells except for meals and weekly recreation periods. "You don't know what it does to a man's nerves to just go from here to the chow hall," growled a resident of one of the windowless four-man cells. "I've gained forty goddamn pounds." But another inmate in similar circumstances observed, "This is the penthouse compared to the Transit Building."

The Transit Building, a three-story structure within the walls of the penitentiary, is the place where new inmates wait for a bed to become available in one of the regular institutions. Some have waited for five months; others have waited ten. Inmates housed there have little to do but watch television. They are not even allowed to play cards, since

7

officials fear it would lead to gambling and even more fights than they already have. In a second-floor dormitory, 140 inmates have lived in a space designed for 40. The entire building usually holds over 300 men. The Transit Building "is the abomination of this institution," according to Acting Warden Bob Morford. Charles Bass, assistant commissioner, said, "My number one priority is to get money to allow us to close the Transit Building down."

Ancient bastions are not the only places where overcrowding hurts. Many an administrator has seen his hopes and dreams for a model correctional institution go down the drain when a new facility was swamped by inmates. South Carolina's Kirkland Correctional Institution was overcrowded the day it opened in 1975, and due to a shortage of funds it didn't have enough staff to handle even its rated capacity of 448 inmates. A new center for youthful offenders in Tennessee has had about 80 inmates living in a game room.

Women's institutions have also been affected, as the number of women being sent to prison has shot up in most states. South Carolina designed its new women's prison in the early seventies for 96 women; that was thought to be plenty of room at the time. In December 1975 the institution held 237 women. Missouri had housed 130 women in an eighty-bed institution, but after the superintendent was stabbed in a disturbance, additional housing was found. Most officials attribute the rise in the number of women in prison to the recession. They note that most of the crimes committed by women are nonviolent and economically oriented—passing bad checks and petty theft.

Overcrowding, understaffing and idleness only aggravate a problem that has become endemic to the American megaprison: violence. Most of the nation's large prisons were built at a time when their inmates accepted imprisonment with equanimity. Fights and defiance of guards were rare. Most prison administrators would agree with Delbert Jackson, director of the District of Columbia prison system, who said that ten years ago his inmates were for the most part over thirty years old, convicted of property crimes, and while in prison, "passive and docile." Today, he said, most are convicted of violent crimes and are "far more aggressive, far more sophisticated in the street sense. There are far more young people [the average age in District prisons has been twenty-two], young people who feel they've been abused in the past and you get this striking out."

Officials in California, where the problem of violence has been most severe, have contended that there has been a fundamental change in the personality of the inmates who were being sent to prison in more recent years. The officials said that so many lesser offenders—the petty crooks, car thieves, check forgers—have been distilled out of the prison population by community corrections programs, that most of those remaining constitute the violent hard core. "It took us too long to realize that we're dealing with a different breed of cat," said Philip Guthrie, assistant commissioner of the California Department of Corrections.

Over the last few years California has taken extremely strong measures to try to stem a tide of violence that has left hundreds of inmates and guards wounded or dead. California's most troubled institution—perhaps the most violent prison in America—has been the state prison at San Quentin.

San Quentin prison has dominated the otherwise picturesque little town of the same name since 1850. The prison stands high on a promontory overlooking San Francisco Bay. In mid-1976 it held 2,000 inmates, down from 3,000 a year before.

San Quentin, according to one high-ranking guard, is the

"garbage dump" of the California state prison system. It has been the place where the twelve other state prisons have sent their most hardened and troublesome inmates, he said. There have been so many stabbings, killings and other disturbances at San Quentin that the San Francisco newspapers hardly bother to report them any more, except in two-paragraph items on inside pages.

Two Mexican-American gangs, known as the Mexican Mafia and the Nuestra Familia, have been blamed for most of the violence. Officials said the feud began in 1968 when the two groups were vying for control of the drug traffic inside the prison. Since then it has degenerated into a blood war, with each new killing or stabbing in retaliation for the last. Other violence has been attributed to a white group which calls itself the Aryan Brotherhood. It is said to be made up mainly of imprisoned members of California's notorious motorcycle gangs and to be a successor to a Nazi group that once functioned in the prison. Members of the Brotherhood allegedly have hired themselves out as "hit men" for the Mexican Mafia. And there has been yet a fourth group, the Black Guerrilla Family, which officials said has been responsible for the killing of several guards.

San Quentin officials have taken extraordinary security measures to try to stem the violence. The inmates' every movement is watched by armed guards from "gunwalks" that traverse the cellblocks and exercise yards. On any given day, at least two hundred men are locked in San Quentin's three segregation units. This group is generally composed of prisoners who have been accused of assaulting guards or other inmates, or those whose own lives are in danger and who have requested protective custody. Also, as of mid-1976, there were fifty men in San Quentin under sentence of death.

The men in the segregation units—officially known in California as "adjustment centers"—spend twenty-three

hours a day in their cells. They are let out—one at a time
—for an hour a day to exercise, and once a week for a
shower. Before any man is removed from one of the units
for a review of his status or to meet with his lawyer, his hands
are handcuffed behind his back or to a belt around his waist.
The cuffs are not removed until he is returned to his cell.
There are no programs and no work assignments for these
men. However, they are allowed to request books from the
prison library or individual tutoring from prison teachers.
One of the many men serving his entire term in segregation
is Sirhan Sirhan, assassin of Robert F. Kennedy. Sirhan has
been a "model inmate," said one guard, but "he wouldn't
last twenty minutes" if he were assigned to the general
prison population.

Attempts at Reform

Prison reformers, and prison administrators, have long advocated the closing of the oldest and most obsolete penal
institutions. During the late sixties and early seventies, when
prison populations were way down, this finally seemed possible. But by 1976 it appeared that not only would the old
institutions remain in use indefinitely but also that many
new facilities would be necessary—at an estimated cost of
from $30,000 to $50,000 per bed.

No institution has been condemned as obsolete more
often than the Trenton State Prison in New Jersey. Built in
stages between 1836 and 1907, it covers an entire block in
a working-class neighborhood in south Trenton. It is viewed
by reformers and administrators alike as the antithesis of
everything a modern correctional facility should be. The
atmosphere of the huge stone prison is reflected by a plaque
on the façade of the original building, constructed in 1799
and now used to house the superintendent and his family.
LABOUR, SILENCE, PENITENCE, it reads.

11

The prison has been condemned again and again, over the last fifty years, as unfit for human habitation. Dr. Lloyd McCorkle, former commissioner of New Jersey's Department of Institutions and Agencies, once denounced Trenton as "nothing but a mishmash of the worst antique ideas on prison construction dreamed up in the last two hundred years."

Eighty-eight cells that form one wing were built in 1836 to hold one man each. They have held as many as four in the past, and have recently held two or three. They are dark, airless little rooms that one must stoop and descend two steps to enter, with solid steel doors instead of bars.

Most of the inmates at Trenton are housed in three-, two- and one-man cells stacked four tiers high. There is little air or light, and due to faulty heating and ventilation, the cells are chilly in winter and stifling in summer. Since to be sent to Trenton is considered an added punishment, the penalty for failing to "adjust" at the state's other, less secure prisons is transfer there.

Until a few years ago there was no vocational training at Trenton, and the academic program involved only a handful of inmates. Programs have since been expanded, but still are attended by a minority of inmates. The rest do what Trenton inmates have always done: they work at maintenance and janitorial chores, they labor at several prison industries, or they do nothing. Harsh living conditions and idleness have generated extreme tension. Stabbings, fistfights, homosexual rapes, suicide attempts and other disturbances have been commonplace.

After Commissioner of Institutions and Agencies Ann Klein took office in 1974, she promised to close Trenton. "I'm not willing to administer that kind of monstrosity," she said, "so I have to close it." But the prison has outlasted many an administrator who made the same promise. Commissioner Klein succeeded in reducing the 1,300-inmate population of the prison by about one-third. She also closed one cellblock, built in 1886, and to ensure that it wasn't reoccupied, she had the cells ripped out. But according to officials, dismantling will go no further. In mid-1976 all the other prisons in the state were jammed with inmates, about a hundred were backed up in the county jails, and there was no prospect that the state legislature would appropriate money to build a new facility. Unless a new prison is eventually built, there is every chance that the nineteenth-century Trenton State Prison will be around to greet the twenty-first century.

It was not many years ago—no more than twenty in most states—that American prison inmates lived a mechanical existence in which their every freedom was denied. Their heads were shaved. They were forced to wear prison uniforms. They were marched in formation from activity to activity. Their mail was heavily censored. Their rights to reading material and visits from outside were sharply restricted.

During the last ten years—sometimes with the help of the courts—the regimen in most prisons has been considerably relaxed. Long hair, beards and mustaches are so common among younger inmates that they have almost become a new kind of uniform. Inmates are, within limits, permitted to wear civilian clothes of their own choosing. Many who can afford it, or who have generous relatives on the outside, have their cells equipped with radios, televisions and stereos. Censorship of mail has for the most part been eliminated. Visiting rights have been vastly expanded. And in most states inmates are permitted to read almost anything they wish.

One state—liberal Minnesota—has institutionalized these changes and turned them into a philosophy. It is known as the "justice model" of corrections, a phrase that

13

become director of field services for the department. He has two master's degrees. When Fogel sent him back to the prison as warden in 1971, he recalled in an interview in his Stillwater office, "I found devastation here." There was "complete demoralization of staff, hopelessly numb middle management, unlimited visitation by outside groups." The inmates were to a large extent running the prison, McManus added, and he had to struggle "to keep her from going under—retaining control and security." He said that he has spent several years "doing a lot of bailing water."

McManus' main complaint against Fogel was that "he didn't make any preparation for the changes. He just said, 'Do 'em!' We're still picking up the pieces."

Fogel, in response, said that if the changes he ordered resulted in chaos, it was because of poor implementation by the prison staff.

Despite his criticism of Fogel's methods, McManus is sympathetic to his goals. "I do not much want to be the old independent warden-king," he said. But by relinquishing some of his power, he added, he forced some of the weaker inmates to fend for themselves. "What's happened is that the domination by the benevolent despot warden has been replaced by an environment that permits inmates to hurt each other more than they should. The openness would scare me if I were an inmate in here. I can eliminate that by going back to more lockup time. But this is tolerable. . . . The number of assaults compares favorably to other prisons. The drug traffic [in 1975] is as great as in any state, but less than it was two years ago."

The smuggling of drugs and alcohol into the prison has been a political issue for years. It was due to constant protests from the legislature and newspaper editorials that the visitation program for relatives and friends was cut back by McManus and Commissioner Schoen. In a talk before a community group Schoen made an extraordinary admission:

he acknowledged that some of the drugs and liquor were being brought into the prison by guards.

Another unforeseen result of opening up the prison was a rash of suicides. By late 1974, suicides had become so common that the inmate newspaper, *The Prison Mirror*, began to treat them lightly. In its September 27, 1974, issue, the *Mirror*, which is completely inmate-run and uncensored, ran a story describing an unsuccessful escape attempt by six inmates. "In another tragic indiscretion," the story continued, " 'Doc' Sporleder, using very little rope, escaped by hanging himself."

McManus considered the suicides inevitable in the more tense, unstable atmosphere of the open prison, where the strong inmates could more easily victimize the weak. The tragedy, McManus added, was that "I don't know that the inmates are any better off [in the open prison]."

Many other prisons around the country have tried to liberalize their internal operations. Generally only very small institutions—with no more than 200 to 300 inmates—have been able to institute such reforms without causing administrative and security problems.

One disastrous effort was started in 1972 at the Massachusetts Correctional Institution at Walpole. On January 20, 1975, a team of six prison guards entered Cellblock A-1. They were wearing riot gear, with flak vests, helmets and face shields. They approached a cell and told the inmate he was being transferred to another section of the prison. He refused to go and slipped a "pin" into the lock of his door so that it could not be opened from the outside.

The guards finally had to break open the door. The inmate resisted, and they had to drag him kicking and screaming out of the cellblock. While the struggle was going on, someone shouted "Rip out!" and a number of other prisoners began tearing their cells to pieces, ripping out the sinks

17

and toilets and hurling pieces of porcelain, unopened cans of food and other debris at the officers as they retreated.

During the next five days, two teams of guards moved more than two hundred inmates, many of them forcibly, from the A section of the maximum-security prison to the B section. For more than two weeks the inmates in B section conducted what was later called a "controlled riot." As soon as they were moved into their new cells, they immediately ripped out the plumbing and hurled pieces of it at any passing officer. The cellblocks were knee-deep in water that had poured out of broken fixtures. Inmates defecated on the floor of their cells and threw the feces at officers or the cellblock wall. They urinated in cups and threw the urine at officers, who ended up having to wear rain gear and hip boots when they walked through some cellblocks. When the inmates ate they would throw the garbage on the floor.

As quickly as the guards could clean up the mess, the inmates created a new one. Eventually the prison administration gave up, and in some of Walpole's cellblocks, food and human waste from the January 1975 disturbance was still sticking to the walls in September.

The January riot was the last hurrah for the inmates of Walpole prison. For almost three years they had been permitted to run what many considered a de facto experiment in self-government. It is generally agreed that the guards had completely lost control of the prison sometime early in 1972, and there were long periods of time when they even refused to enter the cellblocks. At one point they walked out on strike.

The inmates were governed from 1972 until January 1975 by what is thought to be the only officially sanctioned inmate union in U.S. prison history. It was called the National Prisoners Reform Association (NPRA). Prison guards, and some disgruntled inmates, charged that the NPRA would be better described as a gang of ruthless thugs whose leadership

18

literally terrorized Walpole's five hundred inmates.

During the three-year period the NPRA was in power, prison officials said, there were fifteen inmates murdered at Walpole, and hundreds of guards and inmates were stabbed, assaulted with pipes and beaten by a small group of prisoners who roamed freely about the facility. Some inmates died when their cells were "torched" by their enemies. Others were thrown off tiers. It was during this period that Albert DeSalvo, who confessed to being the Boston Strangler, was found dead in his cell at Walpole with nine stab wounds in his chest. Many of these crimes, officials said, were committed by inmates frenzied with drugs. Narcotics were flowing freely into the prison because of liberalized visiting rules granted by the administration in negotiations with the NPRA.

Whenever the prison administration tried to crack down on the violence, a riot broke out. During one eighteen-month period there were two major riots in which inmates took complete control of the prison, and a half-dozen lesser disturbances. Everything that would burn was burned, and everything that would break was broken.

Much of the blame for this chaos was placed on John O. Boone, the reform-oriented administrator who took over as commissioner of corrections in January 1972. Boone contended that the violence was a direct result of sabotage by some guards and elements of the guards' union, who, he said, were willing to go to any lengths to resist his attempts to loosen up the rigid rules that had governed life at Walpole. Boone said he "encouraged the inmates to organize" in order to give them more responsibility for their own behavior and programming.

Boone was under orders from then-Governor Francis Sargent to "reform" the operation of Walpole and to institute new rehabilitation programs. Boone said that after taking one look at the maximum-security prison, he concluded that the only possible reform was "to tear the goddamn place down." His plan, he said, was to "depopulate it, let it hang there, point to the cost, and then close it."

Meanwhile, Boone wanted to abandon what he considered to be an overemphasis by guards on custody and security. The guard force totally controlled the operation of the prison, Boone recalled. When he tried to take away some of their authority and give the inmates more responsibility for their own behavior, many guards rebelled, Boone said, by refusing to do anything at all. All of the troubles at Walpole, he added, could be traced to the fact that the "guards stopped guarding."

The guards responded that they had refused to cooperate with Boone because they were in fear for their lives. So many of them were assaulted during the Boone period, they maintained, that many of the best officers quit or would do their tours of duty only in the prison towers.

Oddly enough, when the guards walked out for fourteen days in May 1973, there were few incidents inside the prison. Prison reformers point to this period as proof of Boone's contention that prisoners were capable of governing themselves, that they didn't need to be so heavily guarded.

Governor Sargent fired Boone in June 1973, and a state police colonel took over Walpole.

A succession of new wardens failed to stem the violence. Finally, in 1975, the new commissioner, Frank Hall, appointed an official from the North Carolina prison system, Frank Gunter, who quickly came to the conclusion that "our options were to lock the place up and leave it locked up, or to divide it up." Every inmate in the institution was screened and briefly interviewed, then assigned to either the A or B section of the prison. The A section was designated "medium" security, and inmates assigned to it were permitted to live a normal prison life—to work, take educational courses, have regular visits and participate in work-release and furloughs. Those in the B ("maximum") section of the prison were denied all this. They spent all but an hour a day locked in their cells.

Gunter also adopted what he called the "work ethic" at Walpole. He said some of the inmates had not done any work at all in years, but when he took over, all inmates in the A section were required to work in prison industries. Any inmate who refused was moved to the B section. And any inmate in the B section, even if he was cleared as a security risk, also had to agree to work before he could move to the A section.

By early 1976 Walpole prison was, if anything, more custody- and security-conscious than before Boone's administration. "Morale among the [300] officers is one hundred and fifty percent better," said Fred Butterworth, deputy superintendent for operations. Butterworth credited Warden Gunter with "taking positive action to get things stabilized the way they should be."

For the most part, American prison inmates are poor. About 40 percent are black, Puerto Rican or Chicano. Their average educational attainment is sixth grade or below. Depending on the state, 10 to 20 percent of them are totally illiterate. Few have any job skills; in fact, many of the younger offenders have never held a steady job in their lives.

Most prison administrations try to address these problems. By far the most common prison programs are remedial; others provide academic and vocational training. In few prisons, however, do such programs reach more than 25 percent of the inmates who need them. Prison vocational instructors and school principals have complained for decades that when the prison budget is cut, educational programs suffer first. They add, however, that prison reformers who say that such programs should involve almost all inmates ignore the fact that many inmates who would ben-

21

efit by improving their education are simply not interested. Said Raymond Procunier, former director of the California Department of Corrections: "I wonder why everybody expects the minute a guy is convicted and sent to state prison, then the guy's attitude is going to be good—he wants to go to school, he wants to do all [those things] that society couldn't get him to do out there with all the good people." Critics of the prison system have said that a lot more inmates would be interested in educational programs if they were paid for attending. Many inmates without other resources forgo educational programs to take paying jobs, usually in prison industries, which most administrators acknowledge are of little value vocationally. And though a few states have instituted work programs in which inmates can earn as much as $100 a month, prison pay is usually very low—seldom more than a dollar a day, and often much less.

If there has been a growth industry in the prison business, it has been in psychiatry and psychology, not education. Over the last decade there has been an explosion of programs to treat inmates deemed mentally ill—inmates who twenty years ago would simply have been thrown together with the general prison population to cope as well as they could. Nevertheless, prison administrators have complained that the level of available psychiatric care is still woefully inadequate. Few prisons have more than one or two psychiatrists, and these men and women often spend most of their time screening new admissions and preparing reports for parole boards.

There is, however, one kind of prisoner who has gotten more sustained attention from psychiatrists and psychologists than others—the sex offender. Several states, including Minnesota, California, Washington and Massachusetts, have special statutes mandating that sex offenders receive special psychiatric treatment. One of the oldest statutes is in effect in New Jersey, which passed a Sex Offender Act in

1947. New Jersey sex offenders sent to prison under that law have participated in one of the most unusual treatment programs (described below) in the country.

"Well, what happened was, I met this person and we became like really great friends," said Lennie, a freckle-faced man with a great shock of red hair who looks younger than his twenty-seven years. One night he and his girl friend went out drinking, he continued, and "as we were going back to the apartment we went into the elevator and I just got this urge to sock her up and I didn't have any specific reason to . . . I beat her. I poked her face up pretty good, ya know, because she was just a tiny little thing . . . I actually raped her on the elevator and then when the elevator stopped on my floor I took her out, took her into my room, and I raped her in there and in the hallway. And then I was ready to let her go, ya know. And I went past this community bathroom which was like the dirtiest place that I have ever seen in my life, ya know, and that's where the last rape *had* to take place. . . .

"And then I drove her to the hospital and left her off."

That was Lennie's first rape, and it was so violent and unexpected that "it scared even me." After that it was much easier, he said, though his victims were strangers—"housewives that were going about their daily routines."

Lennie (not his real name) was finally caught and sentenced to thirty years in prison. He would be the first to admit that at that time he was a very sick and very dangerous man. In 1974, after serving five years of his sentence, he was released—"cured" to his own satisfaction and that of New Jersey prison officials. He has been in no trouble with the law since his release.

Lennie went into a therapy program at the Rahway Treatment Unit (RTU) for sex offenders at Rahway State Prison. He has been considered one of the best examples of the

23

effectiveness of a special treatment program called ROARE
—Reeducation of Attitudes and Repressed Emotions. Developed by clinical psychologist and RTU director William Prendergast, ROARE has been used at RTU since 1967.

Through ROARE, says Prendergast, rapists and child molesters can plumb the depths of their subconscious in search of the source of their compulsive and aberrant sexual behavior and learn to control it. ROARE treatment methods have profoundly changed dozens of sex offenders whom conventional therapies would never have reached, Prendergast maintains.

The main purpose of the ROARE therapy is to uncover and analyze the psychological wounds and past sexual traumas of the sex offender, which Prendergast believes are the source of many sex crimes. Seventy-five percent of the inmates who have been through his program, he says, were themselves sexually abused as children, often so brutally that they have repressed the memory.

Lennie was not an unusual case. One night when he was six years old, he recalled, "my stepfather came in drunk with a bunch of the fellows from work . . . and they were all really zonked out of their minds and they started crackin' on me for sex. . . . When they tried to hold me down to perform their acts for them . . . I tried to fight them off. [So] they had their sex forcibly. . . . And then I found out where my mom was really at because she continued the sex act that night with me." For years afterward, Lennie's parents continued to abuse him sexually. He finally escaped from home by committing a series of crimes for which he was sent to a state training school.

Years later, when Lennie was committed to the Rahway Treatment Unit, he had only a vague memory of being sexually abused as a child. The ROARE treatment methods forced him to recall these incidents. With Prendergast's help he interpreted his urge to rape as an expression of

24

intense, almost murderous hatred for his mother.

Lennie did not come by such insights without pain. It took years of brutal, emotion-charged ROARE sessions before he and Prendergast concluded that the "gruesome, creature-like thing" that had possessed him was finally gone.

The ROARE program has been voluntary because its effectiveness depends upon the full cooperation of the inmates. More than half of the offenders in RTU have volunteered for ROARE. Prendergast says many have done so because they thought it would help them to be released sooner.

The ROARE treatment—and for that matter, all treatment at RTU—proceeds from a set of assumptions that Prendergast says were drawn from his eight years of experience with sex offenders. The most important of the assumptions is the idea of "compulsion." The most striking characteristic of the sex offenders in the Rahway Unit has been that "fewer than one percent have any idea why they committed their crime," the director says, and adds that when they rape a woman or molest a child or repeatedly expose themselves in public, they are driven by unconscious urges beyond their comprehension or control.

The task of Prendergast and his staff is first "to find out what this compulsion consists of" and then to treat it. The purpose of therapy is to force the inmate/patient to dredge up the "repressed" hatred, fear and insecurity that led to his crimes. Often the principal source of a lifetime of mental torture and sex crimes will be a single incident or series of incidents in early childhood. The terror-stricken child immediately "represses" these incidents, but they continue to act on his subconscious and contribute to his abnormal sex drives.

Conventional individual and group therapy is a slow, arduous and inefficient way of uncovering repressed incidents, Prendergast says. ROARE goes a step beyond these methods, he asserts, in a deliberate attempt to stir the emotions and force the sex offender to recall his sexual past. When the ROARE process works as it should, Prendergast maintains, it transcends the rational, conscious revelations of conventional group therapy and becomes an almost mystical experience for the inmate, with all the frenzied emotion of a rite of exorcism.

The inmate is not purged of his sexual devils simply by remembering the traumas of his childhood, but by reliving them. "He [the inmate] won't be there in the room with us," Prendergast says. "He will be at the place and time and age when the incident happened and he feels, smells, and experiences it. We brought one man back to . . . six months [of age], where he lost urinary and fecal continence, went into a fetal mold, sucked his finger, and babbled."

What makes the ROARE treatment different from other popular group therapies is that inmates run the sessions. "There is total patient responsibility, giving him no cop-outs. He can't blame the therapist, the group, or anybody else, because it's his treatment. He's the captain of the ship. It goes where he wants it to go."

Inmates sometimes drop out of the therapy sessions for weeks or months at a time. Prendergast has them sign a waiver of their statutory right to treatment, and they begin therapy again when they are ready.

All ROARE sessions are conducted in a special room. There is no furniture, only a carpet. Inmates sit on the floor; chairs and other furniture would inhibit free expression, Prendergast explains.

There is no professional therapist in the room. It was discovered early in the program that the presence of a therapist intimidated and inhibited the inmates. Instead, the inmates choose therapists from among themselves. Prendergast and the four other professionals who supervise the therapy watch the sessions, which are video-taped, over a monitor in a nearby office.

The trust between an inmate and his patient/therapist is essential, especially for the inmate with perversions that he would normally never reveal to anyone.

In the ROARE sessions, Prendergast says, "there is no stigma to crying, or to saying, 'I'm afraid,' or to saying, 'I couldn't satisfy a woman.'" The inmates are encouraged to lay aside all their inhibitions. The ROARE sessions, for instance, usually include a great deal of touching—holding hands and hugging. It is only when inhibitions are discarded that a patient will feel totally free to talk about his past and become able physically to experience the "regressive phenomenon" that is the primary goal of the treatment.

Video-taping of all ROARE sessions is a crucial part of the therapy. When an inmate relives a traumatic incident from his past, it is almost always forgotten again, and the patient will have no memory of what happened to him or what he said and did. It is necessary for the inmate to remember the incident for the session to have any lasting therapeutic value. Therefore, he is shown a video tape of the session—if he wants to see it—over and over again "until the memory flows in."

"The patient immediately after his session writes an evaluation of what happened," Prendergast says. "He then sees the tape within seventy-two hours and writes a second evaluation without the availability of the first. If you read the two, you wouldn't believe the difference between what he thought happened and what happened."

Often a patient will "short-circuit" in the middle of a regression and go into a violent rage. Usually the patient is then restrained by the other members of his group. "The rage is uncontrollable and they're unconscious of the direction it's going so we have to control it," Prendergast says.

27

Occasionally, if he knows the patient is not going to attack anyone, he will be allowed to act out. In a tape that has been widely shown to state officials, Lennie lapses into an hysterical rage in which he viciously attacks a body-bag set up in the treatment room. Lennie continues punching the bag, which he perceives as his mother, until he collapses in exhaustion.

Before being considered for release, each offender must first satisfy his staff therapist that he understands the reasons he committed his crime and is unlikely to repeat it. If the therapist recommends parole, Prendergast has the right to veto the recommendation if he thinks the inmate is not ready. If Prendergast agrees to recommend parole, the inmate's application then goes to a special review board made up of psychiatrists and psychologists. It is the duty of the board to review each sex offender's case every six months. If the review board agrees that the offender is ready for parole, it will send his application to the parole board.

During the last several years the RTU staff and offenders have had to contend with a conservative parole board which has been unwilling to release many offenders without absolute assurances that they will not commit sex crimes again.

Prendergast's response has been that "with a lot of these men you're never going to have absolute proof that the urges [to commit sex crimes] won't continue." But those who have completed the program and been released have an excellent record of success, Prendergast said.

Official statistics show that of the more than 400 men who were paroled from the RTU unit as of early 1976, 8 percent had returned to prison, including only 1 percent for new sex crimes. ROARE participants generally had the most severe problems. Of them, the statistics maintain, fewer than 2 percent had returned to prison, including less than 1 percent for new sex crimes.

The ROARE program has forced its subjects to suffer great mental, and sometimes physical, anguish. Its administrators would have argued that this was necessary for the program to be effective. But during the late sixties and early seventies there was growing concern among civil-libertarians that such programs went beyond the bounds of "treatment" and into the nether world of "behavior modification."

Almost any prison program can be defined as behavior modification, in the sense that all of them try to steer offenders away from criminal behavior and into law-abiding behavior. What civil-liberties groups are concerned about, however, is a more narrow range of programs that involves what psychologists call "aversive conditioning." Such a program was operating until 1975 at the maximum-security prison in Somers, Connecticut. The program was suspended in May 1975 after its director, psychologist Roger Wolfe, resigned. As of mid-1976, the program had not been resumed, but Connecticut Corrections Commissioner John Manson said it would start up as soon as qualified staff could be found to run it.

The program, confined to the treatment of child molesters, used electric shock as its main treatment method. The subject would lie on a couch facing a movie screen, his trousers and undershorts pulled down to his knees. A disc attached to a battery-powered device that produces shocks was strapped around his upper thigh, as close as possible to the genitals.

A trained programmer would show slides of young boys or girls, and then of adult men or women (depending on the inmate's sexual preferences), in provocative poses. If the inmate became sexually aroused when the picture of the child appeared, the programmer would give him a harmless but painful electric shock. "At the end," an inmate in the program said, "they always show a picture of an adult and

29

ask you to picture yourself in a sexual situation with her. . . . I know when there is a picture of an adult I won't get a shock.

"I don't like going in there," the inmate continued, "but I know if I don't, I will just keep on doing these things and come back [to prison.] I just keep pushing myself."

The repetition of the treatment over a period of months, Wolfe said, should completely repress an inmate's ability to think of children as sex objects. The inmate comes to think of adults as "relief from pain," he added, because no shock is associated with them.

Wolfe and Connecticut prison officials insisted that the program was completely voluntary and that eligible offenders were given several weeks of orientation before they were permitted to participate.

But the Connecticut Civil Liberties Union filed suit to have the program stopped. William Olds, head of the civil-liberties group, said that the program "smacks of something out of *Clockwork Orange.*" If such programs are permitted to go on, he added, "institutional torture is right around the corner."

Olds also argued that the program was not really voluntary, since the state parole board admitted that it would be more likely to consider parole for a sex offender who had been through the program than one who hadn't. That introduces an element of coercion, Olds claimed.

But the elimination of the program was the last thing that many of the inmates participating in it wanted, since they recognized that they might never get out of prison without it. One inmate who had completed the treatments said that it was a "good program," and would help him to stay out of trouble when he was released. "I think I would really get sick if I did it [molested a child] again," he said. "When I do have those thoughts my stomach gets upset. If I was let out now, I don't think I'd have any trouble."

Chapter 2
Handling Inmate Grievances

In the world of prisons, complaints are as numerous as bars. For most of the last two centuries, however, prison administrators have wielded virtually unchallenged authority over the inmates committed to their custody. Changes have been extremely slow in coming.

Publicity sometimes paves the way for change. Among the actions that gain attention are some that are seemingly senseless and self-destructive. At Louisiana's Angola prison, in 1959, an inmate cut off his own testicles, according to prison medical records, and handed them to a guard. He told doctors that he didn't "feel like a man" after years in confinement, and therefore had no further need for those organs.

However, the action that consistently gains the greatest public attention is the most spectacular: the prison riot. Riots usually start with an isolated incident (a fight among inmates, for instance), but they often end with inmates united to present a list of grievances concerning their living conditions. Riots have occurred with increasing frequency since 1950, the bloodiest being the uprising at New York's

Attica prison in 1971. Nine guards and thirty-four inmates were killed.

The Attica tragedy thrust prisons into the light of public scrutiny, and it spurred many proposals for reform. This does not mean that prior to Attica, prisoners had made no progress, nor that prison administrators made changes only when confronted by a riot. The field of prison administration has changed considerably, with state departments of corrections being formed to administer previously autonomous institutions. Sometimes these departments have been headed by people with backgrounds in politics or teaching; sometimes administrators have been named who had reputations as "prison reformers." But in many cases administrators have seen their reform proposals and their pleas for adequate funding rejected by state politicians, who seem mindful of a former Louisiana governor's dictum that "There ain't no votes in prison."

In the last few years, inmates have discovered a more peaceful, and often more successful, avenue of protest than rioting: the lawsuit. Whereas at one time prisoners' suits were summarily dismissed, in recent years judges have examined almost every facet of prison life to see if it conforms to constitutional standards. A flood of inmate lawsuits, some of them frivolous, have resulted—to the dismay of judges and administrators alike. Some overworked judges complain that a lawsuit should not be necessary to determine such issues as permissible hairstyles for inmates.

Many administrators agree. They have discovered that both riots and litigation can be avoided if complaints are resolved within the prison. Many kinds of procedures have been established to deal with grievances. Some of these procedures involve the inmates themselves. The effectiveness of inmate input was demonstrated in several Southern states in the last decade. There, early attempts at integrating prisons often led to bloodshed until the inmates were consulted. In Louisiana, for instance, inmates came up with an idea involving prison "families"—informal groupings of prisoners who look out for one another, a situation common to almost all prisons. The idea was to move such families into integrated cellblocks as a unit, thus maintaining established relationships. There, integration went smoothly.

But not all problems within a prison can be solved by the time-consuming process of negotiations. What do you do, for instance, when black prisoners at a maximum-security institution suspect that someone is out to get them, and a riot is brewing?

Q. Can you say anything about what happened? Everybody at the prison is upset about what happened to you. . . . Did someone do this to you or did you do it yourself?

A. I set the fire myself.

Q. You set the fire yourself? Could you tell me why you set it?

A. I was disgusted.

Q. You were disgusted with your girl friend?

A. I was disgusted with myself. People were talking about me.

Q. Who were the people talking about you?

A. Everybody.

Q. What time did you do this?

A. Between six and six-thirty.

Q. In the morning?

A. It happened yesterday . . . between six and six-thirty in the morning.

Q. What else did you do besides set the fire?

A. I swallowed some Sani-Flush.

Q. You swallowed some Sani-Flush. . . . Did you do anything else?

A. Some Thorazine . . .

Q. Did you do this before you set the fire?
A. Yes. Everything.

The tape recorder in the special burn unit of a Minnesota hospital absorbed all of those questions and answers. The questioner was Theartrice Williams, the dean of a small but growing group of correctional mediators called ombudsmen. As the ombudsman for corrections in Minnesota, he had been called to the prisoner's bedside by the warden of the state's maximum-security prison at Stillwater.

It had been an emergency call, fraught with concern because this was the second suicide attempt within the prison in forty-eight hours. Both involved black inmates. One was dead; one was dying.

Behind the walls at Stillwater, some twenty miles away from that hospital room, black inmates were angry. They, as well as some prison staff members, openly questioned how a prisoner could padlock himself in his cell and set it on fire. There was heated talk among the inmates that "they" were out to get the black prisoners. Only two days earlier another black inmate had hanged himself with a bed sheet under what other blacks thought were mysterious circumstances.

Immediately after the bedside interview with the dying inmate, Williams, who is black, drove to Stillwater and met with a group of skeptical prisoners. He played the tape recording. He let them make a copy. Hours later the inmate died, but the tension at the prison was broken as a result of the taped interview.

Such high drama has filled few of Theartrice Williams' assignments. Yet in the long run he and the ombudsmen in other states are facing one of the greatest challenges in American corrections: responding to inmate demands for change.

Ombudsman means "agent" or "representative" in Swedish, and it was in Sweden that this concept of "watchdog" originated, in 1810. There he is an official, appointed by the Parliament, who watches over the performance of all government agencies. He investigates complaints from citizens, and when he finds error or injustice, tries to correct the situation. Several other nations have ombudsmen. In Minnesota, Williams has had responsibility for just one area: prisons. He was appointed by the governor, is answerable to him and is required to report on an annual basis to both the governor and the legislature.

Many consider this independence a key to Williams' success. Connecticut also has an independent ombudsman for prisons; so has Michigan, where the legislature has appointed an ex-inmate. Other states, such as South Carolina, Kentucky, Ohio and New Jersey, have appointed ombudsmen who are responsible to the department of corrections. In those cases the prisoners often mistrust them because, in the words of one inmate, "You can't expect the man to bite the hand that is signing his check."

The degree to which prison staff and inmates initially accept an ombudsman depends largely on the circumstances under which the program was set up. In the long run, however, acceptance depends on the ombudsman's own credibility with two groups: inmates and guards.

At least fourteen states have some sort of correctional ombudsmen. And the ombudsmen generally agree that they operate best where they are an adjunct to an existing grievance procedure that winnows out and resolves many complaints at a lower level. Some of those other grievance mechanisms will be discussed later.

Williams, the nation's first prison ombudsman, received six inmate complaints at his house before he even opened his office in July 1972. Barely four months after starting work he was called to Stillwater by both inmates and the administration while a prisoner was holding a guard hostage at knifepoint. After several hours of negotiations with the ombudsman, the prisoner handed his weapon to inmate leaders and the incident ended without bloodshed or the administration having to meet unreasonable demands.

But things did not always go so smoothly at the beginning. It took time and several clashes between the ombudsman and prison staff to develop a spirit of mutual trust. Most Minnesota observers agree that the first year of the program was a period of testing and some confrontation.

In reviewing the first year of the program, Warden Bruce McManus admitted that "I was uptight. He [Williams] was uptight. And our staff fought him. We went from suspicious holding off to a serious confrontation. But I think Williams learned a lot. He and I have learned a lot together."

McManus later praised Williams for his "willingness to see both sides. He's a straight professional . . . an honest man. . . . At least he understands our problems and how we think. He may not buy it, but he understands."

The head of the Minnesota corrections system, Commissioner Kenneth Schoen, concurs: "I don't know how we operated without it. Williams is a reasonable man. That's the potential flaw in this system. You're dependent on a nonbiased man with no hidden agenda. . . . Williams happens to be a man without any [biases]."

During the first two years of operation, Williams and his staff dealt with nearly two thousand complaints. Only six were dismissed because they were beyond the legal reach of the ombudsman's office. Virtually all complaints have been handled—from receipt to final disposition—within a month. Slightly more than two-thirds of all complaints have come from the prison at Stillwater, which holds just over half of the state's adult inmates.

While Williams has been interested in solving legitimate individual gripes, he does feel that he really accomplished something significant when he negotiated major policy changes. And he has negotiated them.

- He helped set up an inmate/staff advisory council, which has served as an outlet for grievances.
- His recommendation that a nonprison employee serve as the independent chairman of the inmate disciplinary court was adopted.
- He insisted on and received an accounting of the inmates' welfare fund.
- He negotiated an agreement that provides inmates with written reasons for denial of parole.

In undertaking major reviews, Williams has tape-recorded proceedings, made transcripts, gotten legal help from the state attorney general's office and called witnesses whose names he has kept confidential. His recommendations have been based on this full documentation. In cases where the press had already reported on incidents that prompted an investigation, Williams has made his report public. So that the inmates know what's going on, the ombudsman has condensed his findings and has presented them regularly in the prison newspaper.

Williams cannot order changes himself. He must negotiate most of them with the corrections department, so his success depends substantially on his relationship with the commissioner and with other top officials. Williams can also use the power of public opinion on a specific issue, and as a last resort, he can initiate a court suit.

Williams believes that his prior ignorance of penology was helpful in his early days on the job. "I didn't have any reputation in the corrections field and that may have been the most important asset I brought to the job. A corrections background means the person goes in compromised. . . . He will make some assumptions . . . [and] that's deadly. The other thing that's deadly is the assumption of what cannot be done. It's surprising what you can do when you're not stuck with those hang-ups."

Other Grievance Mechanisms

Using ombudsmen is only one way of responding to prisoners' complaints. Most institutions report that they have some way of resolving the grievances of inmates: inmate representative councils, legal-services programs, arbitration or review procedures within institutional staff structures.

The Center for Correctional Justice (CCJ), in Washington, D.C., has been devoted to studying and promoting grievance mechanisms. The center, a nonprofit organization, was set up in 1971 and has been headed by attorney Linda R. Singer. While CCJ has not advocated one single type of grievance mechanism for all institutions, it has recommended several features. A grievance mechanism, CCJ said, should:

- Include participation by both inmates and staff;
- Be simple to understand and operate;
- Have strict and fairly short time limits for each stage of resolution;
- Provide at some point for review by a person or agency from outside the corrections department.

Juvenile institutions in California use one grievance mechanism that meets many of these criteria. Developed by inmates and staff with the aid of CCJ, it is unlike grievance systems that are based on the adversary model of the courtroom; rather, it is patterned after labor negotiations. An example of its operation is this account of an actual complaint hearing at the Youth Training School in Ontario, California:

Donald B. gets a grievance form, describes his problem in ten typewritten lines and hands it to a grievance clerk, a fellow ward (inmate) whom the other inmates have elected to the post.

Donald then asks one of his buddies to represent him at the grievance-committee meeting. This is on Monday. On Friday afternoon of the same week, the Team E (residential units are called teams) grievance committee meets in the brick-walled visiting room to hear Donald's complaint and those of four other wards.

The committee is composed of two wards (including the grievance clerk), two staff members and a chairman who is a school employee not directly connected with Team E. They sit at the head of a T-shaped arrangement of tables. Along the stem of the T sits Donald and across from him is Richard L., Donald's spokesman.

Richard reads Donald's complaint aloud: "I received a package six months ago with some eight-track tapes and an AC/DC cassette recorder. I was told that we weren't allowed to have them. They were sent back home in two separate packages. My mother received the first package, which was the tapes. The second never arrived." Richard explains that Donald wants an investigation of what happened to the recorder as well as compensation for its loss.

One committee member asks Donald what he has done so far to learn what happened to the missing recorder.

"I tried talking several times to the security officer," Donald says. "He kept writing my name down and telling me he'd let me know, but I never got any results."

Another committee member asks, "Did you get a slip in your mail saying that the package had been sent back to your mother?"

"I was never even notified that the package arrived here. I didn't find out until my mother wrote me that she had sent it."

The grievance clerk recalls that he has received packages

39

of street clothes in the past, which were declared contraband by prison officials. "But I always got a slip saying that the package was being kept in storage and that I could send it back with visitors. I feel that the staff were wrong in not sending [Donald a similar] slip."

Richard agrees. "I would like it stipulated that the responsible party should pay compensation for the recorder."

The committee recesses and moves into the next room to discuss the case privately. After about five minutes the panel reconvenes in open session. "The results of the committee findings are that a lost-package tracer should be initiated," the chairman says. Since AC/DC cassette recorders now are permitted at YTS, he adds that "if the package is not found within thirty days, it should be replaced out of the school's funds.

"Have your mother send a description of the last recorder . . . so that a similar model can be purchased," the chairman concludes. He starts to prepare for the next grievance hearing on the committee's agenda. And with a nod of his head, Donald indicates satisfaction that his grievance has been taken care of.

Had Donald not approved of the result, he could have appealed the decision to a panel that included a professional outside mediator. The panel's decision, however, would not have been binding on the director of the California Youth Authority.

Court Suits

As previously mentioned, inmates can go to court when grievance procedures aren't available or appropriate. Raymond Procunier, who headed the California Department of Corrections from 1968 to 1975, during some of its most turbulent years, dates the beginnings of the prison-reform movement to "about '69, '70. About that time was the first time any attorneys ever came up and knocked on the door and asked us questions. And, man, we were in a panic, because lawyers are almost like psychiatrists when it comes to panicking laymen. Prior to 1967, in all my experience in corrections up to that time, one lawyer had called me up, when I was superintendent at Tracy. He inquired about a guy, wanted to know if he had any money. I said, 'No.' He said, 'Well, f--- him.' "

In recent years, however, administrators and judges have been inundated by lawsuits and court petitions initiated by prisoners. Most of these have been filed in the federal courts —the result of a 1961 decision in which the U.S. Supreme Court ruled, in *Monroe* v. *Pape*, that state prisoners could seek redress in federal courts for alleged violations of their constitutional rights. Some judges have said that the volume of petitions from inmates not only has resulted in long processing time but also has precluded giving adequate attention to any one complaint. Reporting on this matter in 1972, a federal-court study group said that "we are, in truth, fostering an illusion [of thorough judicial review]. What the prisoner really has access to is the necessarily fleeting attention of a judge or a law clerk."

Even worse, many judges have said, is that the large number of obviously frivolous petitions has tended to obscure those complaints that have genuine merit. "Certain prisoners file petition after petition," said one judge, "and it's very easy for a judge to start thinking there is nothing meritorious about any of these claims. You really can't approach [inmate grievances] with that attitude, but it's easy to slip into it. Because you read so many frivolous claims, the good ones are sort of buried."

Judges admit that even when complaints are valid, the court often finds it difficult to effect an appropriate remedy. A judge doesn't have the time to follow up every order to make sure administrators are complying with it. Some judges

41

also believe that prison officials are less responsive to court orders than to the directives of their superiors in the executive branch of government.

Despite these difficulties, the courts have entered a number of strong decrees in favor of inmates. Arkansas, Louisiana and Florida have all had their correctional systems declared unconstitutional—usually because of overcrowded facilities. Most New York City correctional institutions have also been declared unconstitutional.

The focus of the Louisiana case was the state penitentiary at Angola. It gained notoriety as one of America's worst prisons when, in February 1951, thirty-seven inmates slashed their Achilles tendons to protest harsh conditions and brutal treatment. Two tides of penal reform swelled and ebbed in the fifties as a result of such scandals. Another began in the late sixties. Although some improvements were instituted at Angola—such as the abolition of the use of inmates as guards, practiced there from 1917 to 1972—the prison was the target of a sweeping federal court order issued in June 1975. In his opinion, Federal District Judge E. Gordon West wrote that conditions at Angola "should not only shock the conscience of any right-thinking person, but . . . also flagrantly violate basic constitutional requirements as well as applicable state laws."

Judge West's order covered eight specific areas: security at Angola, medical care, maintenance of the physical plant, food and sanitation, racial discrimination, religious freedom, mail censorship and disciplinary due process, including punitive confinement.

In some areas the court order was very specific. For example, 587 correction officers were on the staff at the time of the court order, which declared that the number be increased to at least 950 within six months. (In 1970, there were only 171 correction officers at Angola. A year later there were 460, and the prison augmented this force with

200 inmate-guards.) Judge West also ordered that at least two security officers be assigned to each dormitory twenty-four hours a day; before the order, one or two officers often covered four dormitories. He ordered daily shakedowns for weapons and other contraband; previously, shakedowns were conducted irregularly, depending on "need" and available manpower.

The court order recognized that lack of money was the real obstacle to improvements at Angola. It acknowledged that Corrections Director Elayn Hunt (who died in early 1976) and Warden Murray Henderson had "attempted in good faith to eliminate certain of the conditions the Court has found to be unconstitutional, but have been prevented from doing so, because of the lack or shortage of funds.

"However, shortage of funds is no defense to an action involving unconstitutional conditions and practices. . . . This Court does not order the Louisiana Legislature to appropriate money for prison reform. However, it does require that if the state . . . chooses to run a prison, it must do so without depriving inmates of rights guaranteed to them by the federal constitution."

Many legislators, journalists and others well acquainted with Louisiana politics said that changes of the kind ordered by Judge West would take ten to twenty years to implement. Hunt herself put the figure at ten years.

In January 1976 the Alabama prisons were also declared unconstitutional. U.S. District Court Judge Frank M. Johnson's decision in that case is believed to be the first to set down specific guidelines on what an entire prison system must provide its inmates. The forty-four standards listed in the court order govern all areas of prison life, including visiting privileges, staff composition, living areas, classification procedures, food service, personal hygiene and segregation units.

The judge continued a ban on the acceptance of more

prisoners into the state system until the prison population reached its rated capacity of 2,600. He had issued the ban in August 1975, when the state had 5,100 prisoners; at the time of the January ruling, there were about 4,000. To help implement the standards, the judge appointed a committee of thirty-nine leading citizens, and he authorized them to hire a consultant—at the same rate of pay as the commissioner of corrections.

In the realm of living accommodations, the judge ordered that each man be provided with sixty square feet of living space, and that only minimum-security inmates be housed in dormitories. When he issued the ruling, most inmates were in dormitories. "We don't have a cell in our system which is sixty square feet," said a spokesman for the Alabama Board of Corrections. The few cells the state did have were six feet by eight feet, or forty-eight feet square.

Another major area covered in the order was staffing. The judge ordered that the system, which was 40 percent understaffed even for its design capacity, must make staff increases from the 383 employed at the time to 692. He also ruled that the staff must reflect the racial and cultural make-up of the inmate population.

At the trial before Judge Johnson, a parade of witnesses testified to violence and degradation in the prisons. A prison doctor said after examining the records of two thousand men that he found only forty who had not required medical treatment for a rape or stabbing.

The plaintiffs, assisted by the National Prison Project of the American Civil Liberties Union Foundation and by the Southern Poverty Law Center, brought to the stand nine witnesses to testify as experts, including William Nagel of the American Foundation; Norval Morris, dean of the University of Chicago Law School; John Boone, former commissioner of corrections in Massachusetts; and John Sarver, former commissioner of corrections in Arkansas.

The state conceded that many conditions in the prisons were undesirable, but it pleaded a lack of funds. Matt Myers, one of the ACLU counsels on the case, said Judge Johnson's ruling was stronger than previous federal court rulings against other prison systems in several ways. First, it provided specific standards to be met. Second, he went on, the judge found that Alabama prisons actually made offenders worse, and that the loss of job skills and the deterioration of mental and physical conditions were themselves evidence of unconstitutionality. Third, said Myers, the judge based his ruling not only on the Eighth Amendment standard of "cruel and unusual punishment," but also on the "due process" clause of the Constitution—which, Myers said, could open the door to further suits.

A private attorney who handled one of the original Alabama cases, Bobby Seagall, felt that money alone was not the answer. "I think there were horrible abuses that can't be attributed just to a lack of money," he said, citing practices such as the use of inmates as "strikers" (farm bosses).

It can be argued that in the last fifteen years the lawyers and courts have done more to improve living conditions, and more to narrow the arbitrary decision-making power of guards and administrators, than was accomplished in the previous hundred years by other reformers. Among the rights that have been gained by the inmates are: freedom from mail and literature censorship; expanded visitation programs; access to the courts and media; due process in disciplinary and transfer procedures.

Why did the judges move away from the "hands off" doctrine, under which they had repeatedly ruled that conditions of imprisonment were a matter for politicians and prison administrators to decide, not the courts? Historian David Rothman, in an article in *Civil Liberties Review*, asserts that in cases involving inmates who are Black Muslims "judges found the right [to religious freedom] too traditional, the request too reasonable, and the implications of intervention ostensibly so limited that they had to act. . . . Nor could the courts reject the petitions that followed. . . . Were courts really to stand by helplessly as [some] Arkansas prison guards used the Tucker telephone to give electric shocks to inmates' genitals? Were they going to permit [prisons] to keep convicts for weeks in cells filthy with excrement? Surely institutions could be run without such horrors."

But the process of achieving prison reform through litigation has had its limitations, Rothman and others maintain. The goal of most of the legal organizations involved in prisoner suits has not just been the amelioration of conditions, but the ultimate closing of the prisons. The suits themselves, however, have done little to achieve that goal.

Since its creation in 1972, one of the most active lawyers' groups has been the National Prison Project of the American Civil Liberties Union Foundation, in Washington, D.C. Lawyers from the project assisted in litigating the Alabama suit, and initiated or joined in dozens of other actions across the country. The net result has been improved living conditions and the expansion of inmate rights in numerous prisons, according to project director Alvin J. Bronstein. But there are still just as many people locked up in those prisons. Bronstein hopes that in the Alabama case the judge will ultimately find the conditions so intolerable and so expensive to remedy that he will order at least two of the state's prisons closed, with the release of a substantial number of inmates. But Bronstein admits that even if that happened, it would be a rare case.

"I have been in the business long enough to recognize the limits of the law as an instrument for social change," he says. "It's very limited. Our prime responsibility, and the prime results of our work, will be protecting the day-to-day constitutional rights of the prisoners and upgrading the quality of their lives. It's only when we get a situation where you get a combination of factors like we had in Alabama where we can effect decarceration. But even there, the lawsuit is not going to really have long-range decarceration built into it. That's a political job. That's got to be done from the inside, and from the political community."

When he speaks of decarceration, Bronstein explains, he does not mean that all inmates should be set free. But he believes that in almost every state in the nation the prisons are holding substantial numbers of inmates who would not be a threat to public safety if released. In Southern states like Alabama, he maintains, the proportion may be as high as 75 percent.

Upgrading Corrections Officers

Inmates often direct their complaints against their guards, whom they charge with everything from discourtesy to brutality. Most administrators, while defending their staffs against type-casting, have taken steps to upgrade their personnel. Many departments of corrections have tried to encourage old-line guards to retire. To attract and keep better-qualified staff, including minorities, they pleaded with legislators for higher salaries. Warden Donald Wyrick of the Missouri State Penitentiary feels that low pay in Missouri has led to inexperienced and tired personnel.

In July 1976, the starting salary for a guard was $628 a month. Turnover has been high, averaging about 40 percent annually among guards, according to Warden Wyrick's estimate. He believes that about half of the guards were moonlighting, with a second full-time job. "The man's tired and irritable when he reports to work," he says. "He snaps at the inmate. I know that's true because I did it too. When I was an officer and sergeant I always had two jobs."

47

One state that took major steps to upgrade its corrections officer staff in recent years was Connecticut. Prisons offer starting salaries among the highest in the country—$785 to $975 a month, depending upon qualifications—and the state has also instituted training for officers.

Connecticut corrections officials said that the typical new corrections officer has had fourteen years of education. Not long ago, the only requirement for a guard's position was one year of work experience in any field. Now a high school diploma or its equivalent is also required.

The centerpiece of the state's training program in corrections has been the Connecticut Justice Academy at Haddam. All department employees, except for clerical staff, part-time workers and volunteers, complete four weeks of training, including a period of simulated incarceration designed to make staff more sensitive to the feelings of people who are imprisoned. The location of the academy, used by all criminal-justice agencies in the state for training purposes, is the former Haddam Jail (built in 1786).

In addition to the training course, the department offers college-credit instruction in correctional subjects to thirty-five officers each semester. The state-financed program, involving a full day of classes each week, is available to officers who already have some college credits.

The state of Alaska has tried some unusual methods to help officers empathize with offenders. In one program, corrections officer trainees volunteered to be arrested at an unspecified time in the future and be locked up for a night. "We had the troopers go out and arrest a couple of them and throw them in jail, booked for breaking and entering or lewd and lascivious conduct," Corrections Director Charles Adams recalled. "Those arrested weren't at all sure that it was part of the training program."

They were put in cells, and the standard fifteen-minute checks were run. "You would have the trainee officers coming back to us and saying they'll never slam another cell door, and if anyone asks for a second cup of coffee, he's going to get it."

Chapter 3
Back into Society

On a sunny Saturday morning in Foxboro, Massachusetts, Peter Makarewicz sat down with his mother and sister to a hearty breakfast on the lawn behind their little red house. Afterward he stripped off his shirt, revealing a lean, tanned, well-muscled body, and set to work around the yard. He planted some tomatoes, did some repair work on the driveway and then mowed the lawn.

In the afternoon his mother prepared his favorite meal, pot roast, with strawberry shortcake for dessert. After an early dinner Makarewicz went shopping; he bought a new sports coat and some socks. At 8:30 P.M., after one last piece of strawberry shortcake, Peter Makarewicz went "home"— to Cellblock No. 1, of the Massachusetts Correctional Institution at Walpole, where he was serving a life term for first-degree murder.

Makarewicz had been on furlough, an unsupervised trip into the community. Ten years ago the idea of letting prisoners go free for a weekend, or even an hour, would have struck many people as utter lunacy. But in recent years, more than forty states have instituted furlough programs; an average of seven thousand furloughs have been granted each week to adult prisoners in the United States.

The philosophy behind furloughs is the realization that most prisoners, even "lifers" like Makarewicz, will someday be released from prison to live in freedom; only a tiny minority die in prison. Many penologists see incarceration as a debilitating experience, one which makes it more difficult for an offender to make the right choices outside once he is released. Locking up an offender for a lengthy sentence, and then releasing him with a firm handshake and only bus fare home, often leads to serious problems in making the transition from prison to free society.

Furloughs are only one of the methods that correctional administrators have developed to ease that transition. Work-release programs, which allow offenders to prepare for their toughest challenge, getting a job, constitute another tool. So does parole, which, while heavily criticized by both conservative and liberal criminal-justice professionals, aims to give inmates incentive within prison and assistance upon their release.

Furloughs

Peter Makarewicz was granted his first furlough in 1974, when he was thirty-five years old. He had not been "out" for twenty years.

"The [staff] people in here don't realize what a furlough means to you," Makarewicz said in an interview at Walpole prison. Convicted of strangling a fifteen-year-old girl in 1955, when he himself was only fifteen, he was sentenced to spend the rest of his life in prison. In Massachusetts, offenders convicted of first- and second-degree murder are not eligible for parole. The only way they can ever gain their freedom is to have their sentences commuted by the governor, a complicated procedure that can take years.

51

While Makarewicz knew what the outside world looked like, from television and magazines, he had forgotten what it felt like. "The senses are bombarded by all kinds of impressions. [On my first furlough] I remember walking into [my mother's] house and saying the place looks like a dollhouse. Everything seemed so small. I'm used to wide spaces, long corridors, large dining halls."

During his years in prison, Makarewicz said, he completely lost his sense of what it was like to live in free society; all that he knew about it was from the limited perspective of a fifteen-year-old boy. When he began going out on furloughs, he was "like a guy that had been on another planet half his life and finally came back to a place he once knew."

He said he had to "get used to maneuvering around the furniture and sitting on a couch. Everything was new and strange. Your sense of equilibrium and balance is thrown off. In here [Walpole] everything is streamlined and bare."

One of the greatest pleasures was eating, "to sit and have a cup of coffee in a nice cup," to use regular silverware. The food itself was hard to get used to, because it was so much "richer" than prison fare.

"I'm adjusting gradually, slowly, gaining confidence," Makarewicz said. "I'm beginning to think a lot straighter." He added that he's "not trying to cram everything into these furloughs that I've missed for twenty years. I'm just beginning to learn how to walk into a f-----g store and have enough confidence to ask a guy for a pack of cigarettes."

One of the things he has had to learn to do without is women. But he has resisted the temptation to go out while on furlough and "cop a hoooker," as many men do. "I'm not afraid of women," he said, "but I just feel that I don't have a craving need for it." He added that he would rather wait until he's released and "have a natural, mutual relationship that just happens." While on furloughs, he has met a few young women socially at a friend's house, but has had a difficult time talking to them. "What the hell do you say? I lack confidence in just being myself. I'm afraid I'm going to bore 'em. I don't know how to make small talk. On one furlough I went to the Museum of Fine Arts. That's the only thing I can talk about. But most people have been there."

Peter Makarewicz's mother's hair turned gray within a year after her son was sent to prison. To add to her troubles, her husband became ill shortly after the trial and was only able to work off and on from that time until a few years ago when he died of cancer.

Mrs. Makarewicz said that she could count on one hand the number of Sundays she had failed to visit her son in prison. After a few years, however, both ran out of things to talk about. They would sometimes sit for five or ten minutes without saying a word. "She knows the prison routine as well as I do," Peter said. Mrs. Makarewicz said she would sometimes "talk on and on about things that didn't concern him" just to fill the time. She wasn't interested in the goings-on at Walpole, where her son had been since 1959. "He doesn't tell me anything that goes on inside and I don't want to know," she said.

When Mrs. Makarewicz heard that her son would be coming home on furlough she could hardly believe it, since it had "always seemed so impossible" that it would ever happen. When he is home it is not so hard to find something to talk about. "He's more open and not so depressed since he's been coming home," she said. He also takes some of the burden off her shoulders by doing many of the household chores that she is no longer able to do.

Mrs. Makarewicz believes that her son's performance on furloughs has proven that he is not dangerous and could be released. "He can't undo what he did," she said. "God forgives. He's given enough of his life and now he could come out and do some good in the world."

The governor of Massachusetts apparently agreed with Mrs. Makarewicz. In the fall of 1975 Governor Michael Dukakis commuted Makarewicz's sentence. This meant that he could leave Walpole and live in a co-ed prison. More important, it meant that he could be released on parole in another three years.

Makarewicz was one of about 200 "lifers" in Massachusetts prisons who have gone on regular, unsupervised furloughs into the community. More than 8,000 furloughs were awarded to Massachusetts inmates in 1975.

The use of furloughs has been spreading. A national survey by *Corrections Magazine* found that in 1975, forty-four states and the District of Columbia had provisions for releasing adult inmates on furloughs—also known as home visits, temporary leaves or temporary community release. Forty-five states and the District of Columbia have had furlough programs for juvenile inmates.

During the last few years, more than 30,000 furloughs have been granted each month to adult inmates across the United States, and more than 6,000 to juveniles. Many inmates receive multiple furloughs.

The rapid expansion of furlough programs has represented a veritable revolution in correctional thinking around the country, especially since most states had no furlough program prior to 1969. Before then such programs, at least for adults, were either proscribed by law or used very cautiously and infrequently for carefully screened inmates who needed to go out for some special reason, like deathbed visits, funerals or medical treatment. (In the case of juveniles, home-visiting programs have been in effect for years in some states, though the practice has expanded dramatically in recent years.)

Inmates are permitted furloughs under circumstances that vary from state to state. In a number of jurisdictions, an inmate must give a specific reason for wanting a furlough, such as an employment interview, or a college or vocational school application, or to attend church, to give a talk before some community group, to visit a sick relative, or to attend a son's or daughter's graduation or wedding. Those agencies with the largest furlough programs, however, have sent the greatest number of offenders home simply to visit their families.

Prison administrators do not defend their furlough programs simply as another "goodie" to offer to inmates as a reward for staying out of trouble. Neither are they considered solely a means for relieving inmates' pent-up sexual urges. Instead, administrators generally propose and defend the programs as a means of gradually "reintegrating" an offender into a society that may have become alien to him while he was locked up. Subsidiary benefits of furloughs, they say, are the improvement of morale in institutions and the provision of something tangible for parole boards to look at when deciding whether an offender should be released.

Of all the innovations tried in corrections, furloughs are perhaps the most vulnerable to criticism. Corrections officials have cited statistics showing that over 90 percent of those released on furloughs have returned on time with no problems. But many critics have responded that if even one man on furlough commits a serious crime during his leave, then corrections administrators have abdicated their primary responsibility: to protect the public from the men in their charge.

Attention has often been focused on those instances where men on furlough have committed serious crimes. In one state, for instance, an inmate was sent to prison in 1972 for assaulting his wife. In late 1974, he was released on furlough. During the furlough, he returned to his home and allegedly murdered his wife.

Once a furlough program breaks into the headlines, a cutback or reorganization becomes almost inevitable. A full-fledged political battle over furloughs in Illinois was settled only when prison officials adopted new rules which removed the bulk of the state's inmates from furlough consideration. Many other states with furlough programs can cite similar experiences.

Work Furloughs

Work furloughs and education-release programs have probably been even more widespread than the visitation furloughs of the type Peter Makarewicz received.

These programs seem less controversial, since inmates participating are usually near their date of release, and since they are acquiring skills that might keep them from resorting to crime in the future. These inmates commit few new crimes, according to official statistics. But with each publicized incident these programs, too, have felt the force of community opposition.

For several years Washington, D.C., had an extensive work furlough program. But on September 25, 1974, Calvin Smith was arrested by FBI agents at Washington's Union Station. He had a one-way Metroliner ticket to New York and a box under his arm containing a sawed-off shotgun.

Only twenty months before, Smith had been sentenced to a term of twenty-years-to-life in prison for first-degree murder, plus five-to-fifteen years for armed robbery and burglary. When Smith was arrested at the railroad station, he had not escaped from prison. Officials at the D.C. Correctional Complex in Lorton, Virginia, had released him on furlough. In fact, he had been making frequent unescorted trips into the District of Columbia for several months. As "entertainment coordinator" for the Lorton prison complex, his job was to arrange visits to the D.C. prisons by outside speakers, singing groups and other community organizations.

Smith's arrest brought the roof down on the Department of Corrections' inmate furlough program. Under the administration of District of Columbia Corrections Director Delbert Jackson, the furlough program had become the most extensive and liberal in the nation. During fiscal 1974, 886 inmates in D.C. prisons made 38,500 trips into the community—meaning that each inmate spent an average of forty-three days out of prison that year.

These figures do not include the 1,300 inmates admitted during fiscal 1974 to the District's twelve halfway houses. Under the halfway-house program, some inmates went out every day to work or to school. Others were placed on "out-count" status, meaning that they were permitted to live in the community and report on their activities twice a week to the halfway-house staffs. All halfway-house residents are formally classified as inmates until their parole from the facilities.

At the time Calvin Smith was arrested, the furlough program was already under heavy attack. Early in the summer of 1974 two federal grand juries, one in Washington and one in Alexandria, Virginia, had begun investigating allegations that inmates were paying bribes to gain furlough privileges, and that some corrections officers who escorted furloughed inmates into the community were permitting them to make unauthorized stops on the way to their authorized destinations.

Despite the controversy, Director Jackson had steadfastly refused to tighten the rules governing furloughs, which stated simply that any inmate, whatever his crime, was eligible for escorted furloughs if he had attained medium-security status, and could go on unescorted furloughs if he had minimum-security status.

After the Smith incident Jackson announced that he would not consider changing the furlough program unless he

57

got a direct order to do so from Washington Mayor Walter Washington.

But Jackson had not anticipated a reaction from then-U.S. Attorney General William Saxbe. Without consulting Jackson, or any other D.C. city official, Saxbe issued a written order prohibiting the release on furlough of D.C. prisoners convicted of violent crimes who were not within six months of a firm parole date.

Saxbe issued the order after reading of the arrest of Calvin Smith in the press. "I want to get criminals off the streets," he later told a reporter. "I can't go around the rest of the country jawboning for crime reduction if I can't control what's happening in my own backyard."

The Attorney General's action threw the D.C. Department of Corrections into confusion. Did he have the right to issue such an order? Indeed he did, concluded then-D.C. Corporation Counsel C. Francis Murphy. All federal prisoners and all D.C. prisoners, under federal law, are formally committed to the Attorney General's custody. He in turn delegated the authority to run institutions and programs to lower-ranking officials, including Jackson.

A week after Saxbe's order Jackson suspended the furlough program until he and his staff had time to study the qualifications of each inmate then enrolled in it. They soon found that the order, if strictly adhered to, would effectively eliminate the program. Saxbe had defined violent crimes as murder, manslaughter, rape, kidnapping, robbery, burglary or assault with intent to commit any of those crimes. Virtually all of the inmates then in the furlough program, and in the D.C. prison system as a whole, had been convicted of one or more of those crimes.

To prevent the Saxbe order from destroying his program, Jackson looked closely at the Attorney General's instructions and found that Saxbe had specifically stated that violent criminals could not be released except in "exceptional circumstances." Since such circumstances were not explicitly defined, the Department of Corrections came up with its own definition.

. D.C. Corporation Counsel Murphy, who had helped formulate this definition, summarized it as follows: "In order to be eligible to be considered for a furlough, an inmate [convicted of a violent crime] would have to have served 80 percent of his minimum sentence. Then he would have to indicate a strong desire to benefit from the program, and he would have to demonstrate that he had adapted to his prison environment—he's not kicking up his heels every two minutes about something or other—and that from a psychological evaluation there would be no basis to be concerned that he would cause harm to somebody in the community." Under these rules, the furlough program was reduced to about fifty carefully selected men.

Before, at its height, the furlough program had included three types of leave: "evaluative" visits, to test an inmate to see if he was ready for parole; educational furloughs, for a program designed to prepare inmates for and to enroll them in college programs; and "public service" furloughs. The last category was, in effect, work-release furloughs, and they were the most controversial.

A highly publicized program at the Washington, D.C., Technical Institute, where eight to ten inmates worked with mentally retarded children, set the precedent for work-release programs. Shortly after its inception several years ago, dozens of other inmates had come up with other public services they would be willing to perform on furlough. The vehicles for these programs were inmate "self-help" groups. By the time Jackson became director in mid-1973, there were thirty-six such groups at the Lorton prison complex, and almost all of the groups performed both institutional and community services. At one time, over three hundred inmates from Lorton's main prison, the Central Facility, were making periodic trips into Washington in connection with self-help activities. One group of inmates visited schools, churches and community centers to warn young people of the dangers of drug abuse. Another group visited public housing projects, helping with repairs and maintenance, and also working with ghetto youngsters. Other inmates founded a singing group which performed free at various D.C. functions. One of the better-known self-help groups was the Inner Voices, a black repertory theater group that performed all over the metropolitan Washington area.

The self-help groups were the main victims of the Department of Corrections' internal reorganization of the furlough program. Even before Saxbe's order, all but thirteen men at Lorton's Central Facility had lost their furlough privileges because of alleged rule violations. Subsequently the remaining thirteen were also excluded from the program.

An Inmate Business

In 1971 the state of Washington originated another method of involving inmates in the community through work. There, an inmate-owned and -operated reupholstering business called The Bridge, Inc., thrived for almost four years.

Inmates who worked at The Bridge left the state penitentiary at Walla Walla to pick up furniture in need of reupholstering. They worked on the furniture in a two-story workshop building outside the prison walls and then brought it back to the owners. Later the inmates sent out the bills.

The men who picked up the furniture and worked on it were on minimum-security status. They all lived in the workshop building outside the walls. Another group of prisoners being trained for the business worked inside, learning the upholstery trade with tools leased by The Bridge. When an outside member went on parole, an inside member took his place. The prisoners controlled the corporation's board of directors, organized the work, set quotas and standards, and made deliveries and sales trips throughout the state, accompanied by a member of the noninmate supervisory staff (paid for by grant funds). Prisoners were responsible for their own discipline, and played a major role in the selection of workers.

The "heavy-timers" who conceived of the idea and operated the corporation hoped to make money out of it just like any other entrepreneurs. State corrections officials hoped that in the process the prisoners would learn a new way of life. Officials believed the program demonstrated that private enterprise, relying on the strength of a prisoner's own motivation, could dramatically change his personality.

The Bridge folded in 1975. Spectacular crimes such as those that ended the D.C. furlough program did not cause the shutdown, but rather a general lack of leadership and discipline, according to the superintendent of the prison. The last project director traced this breakdown to the loss of the grant funds, which meant that the special custody staff had to be let go and the inmates had to return to the prison each night.

But Oliver Welles, a corrections officer and the last project director, says that he has not given up on the concept. There was $2,000 left when The Bridge was liquidated, and it was earmarked, Welles says, for another, similar project that he hopes might begin in the near future.

Family Visiting

For inmates not permitted to leave the institution to visit the community, corrections administrators have devised ways to bring the community to them. Visiting rooms, for instance, have often been redesigned to permit prisoners to sit with their visitors in a relaxed setting, and even to embrace. Some institutions have provided pay telephones within the cellblocks so that inmates can keep in frequent touch with their families. Then-Warden Garrell Mullaney of Maine State Prison joked that in some cases the telephones were "cruel and unusual punishment," since some inmates are trying to avoid their family responsibilities—but the round-the-clock phone access at that prison has been popular.

Several states use a more dramatic method to help inmates retain contact with their families—the family visiting program, popularly known as "conjugal visiting." Mississippi has had such a program for many years, and in recent years it has been adopted by New York and California.

At San Quentin, California's toughest prison, family visiting takes place in trailers and apartments on the prison grounds. California officials dislike the term "conjugal visiting," since children and parents are allowed to stay with inmates, not just wives. Visits at San Quentin last either nineteen or forty-three hours.

An inmate we'll call James sat down with his wife in the communal living room of a family-visiting house to talk to a visitor while their two-year-old son romped happily on the rug. James, sentenced to one-to-fourteen years for forgery, said the family visiting program has been "the best thing that ever happened" to California prisoners. He said he had received visits for nearly two years. They began when he was classified minimum custody, and he had had two or three a month ever since.

James said he had been married once before when he started another term in prison. He snapped his fingers, indicating that the marriage immediately broke up. "No contact," he said. "Across the table [in the visiting room] it's not real. There is no contact. You've got to be able to touch to maintain romantic love."

Asked whether he thought the program was degrading, James bristled and escorted his visitor to his family's sleeping quarters, which consisted of one large room with a bed, other furniture, and a private bath. "Is this degrading?" he asked. "We are Muslims. We respect our women. If I thought this degraded her, I would never do it."

To those who have said that the family visiting program has been more than any criminal deserves, James replied, "Though we have broken the rules, we're still human. We still breathe and eat and love."

Parole

The final test of an offender's ability to live in the community is parole. Most inmates are paroled before their sentence expires, although in some states many inmates serve their full terms. (In Arizona, for instance, two thirds of those released have "maxed out," or completed their maximum terms.) While inmates equate parole with freedom, special conditions are attached in many cases, such as being forbidden to drink liquor or being required to get permission before marrying or changing jobs. A violation of these rules can send a parolee back to prison. Sometimes the conditions of the parole are so unrealistic, ex-offenders claim, that virtually anyone can have his parole revoked for cause at any time, depending on the mood of the parole officer. On the other hand, some editorial writers and some politicians often point to crimes committed by men on parole as evidence that too many offenders are let out of prison by parole boards. They also charge that supervision is a sham, because many parole officers are overburdened with caseloads of a hundred or more per officer.

Inmates provide some of the shrillest complaints concerning parole. And in some states much of the controversy stems from a single source: the indeterminate sentence. Such sentences, like five years to life, do not fix a specific or flat term. Instead, they give parole boards great leeway to

63

release inmates on the basis of whether or not they have been rehabilitated. In 1975 the state of Maine eliminated the indeterminate sentence in favor of fixed terms. As part of this move, it became the first state in the nation to do away with its parole board, which had been releasing 95 per cent of those who appeared before it.

In Minnesota, almost any inmate chosen at random at Stillwater or St. Cloud would have a long story to tell about how the Minnesota Corrections Authority (MCA), the state paroling agency, had treated him unfairly. Most inmates there have been serving indeterminate sentences of zero-to-five or zero-to-ten years, with release depending on MCA's judgment of the degree to which an offender has rehabilitated himself while in prison. Minnesota's indeterminate sentences have been less vague than those of California, where many offenders have been serving sentences of zero-to-life, but inmates in Minnesota complain that they never know how long they will be in prison, or what they have to do to get out.

MCA Chairman Richard Mulcrone defended the parole system in an interview. In making parole decisions, he said, he has looked "at what a guy has done while he's in our institution to turn around what I saw as [his] flaws when he came in. Has he worked regularly? Has he participated in whatever is available for changing him? Has he worked at all at improving his mind and abilities? . . . And finally, what [parole] plan has he presented?" But ultimately, Mulcrone added, the decision had to be based "on a lot of gut kinds of feelings about when a guy is ready."

Some professionals have not shared this faith in "gut feelings" found in many parole board members across the country. David Fogel, Minnesota's commissioner of corrections from 1971 to 1973, has aroused a great deal of interest with his "justice model" for corrections. This plan would do away with parole and the philosophy of rehabilitation; instead offenders would serve short, flat sentences fixed by statute.

Contract Parole

There have been many attempts to reform parole without doing away with it. One of the fastest-growing experiments in this area is "contract parole." Under this approach, inmates negotiate with the parole board for their release. The inmate promises to do certain things while in prison, such as taking courses and counseling; in return, the board promises to let him out on parole on a certain date if he has fulfilled his part of the agreement. The agreement is formalized in a contract, which both parties sign.

A side benefit of the contract, from the inmate's point of view, is that if the contract calls for his participation in an institutional program, such as vocational training, he is guaranteed a place in it. Otherwise he might not get in, since popular vocational programs are often oversubscribed.

Wisconsin is one of the first states to experiment with contract parole. One key feature is that each institution has a full-time coordinator whose task it is to take the side of the inmate in his negotiations with the parole board and the institution.

Frankie W. was eighteen years old when he entered the Wisconsin State Reformatory in April 1975 to serve a four-year sentence for two counts of armed robbery. After three months at the institution, his turn came to negotiate a contract. Here is an account of an actual negotiating session between Frankie and the reformatory:

Inside the hearing room, two state parole board members and a reformatory staff member spend a few minutes reading Frankie's file. He is asking for a parole contract that will let him out after one year in prison. Finally one board member says, "Who gave this rascal the idea he might be paroled after just one year of a four-year sentence? After he held a knife to the throat of a woman?"

The second member points to dates scribbled on his notepad. "Is there something to work from in this range?"

The first member nods. "Obviously [contract provision] number four is going to require some alteration. [The provision deals with treatment that the inmate agrees to undergo.] This guy ought to be counseled. . . . He's all screwed up!"

Outside, Frankie talks about the coming session. "I'm asking for [parole on] April 23, [1976,] but I think they'll add some time. But if they give me too much, I won't sign. I'll take my chances [instead] on seeing the parole board in six months. Nervous? Kind of. . . . I'm hoping I get fifteen months or so."

Rich Johnson, the contract coordinator, comes over to say they should start. He leads Frankie into the hearing room, introduces him to the negotiating team and sits next to Frankie at one corner of a large square table. The parole board members sit opposite them; the institutional representative from the reformatory staff sits on the fourth side of the table.

Frankie reads, haltingly, from the contract proposal that he and Johnson have worked out in advance:

"I will take an auto mechanics course at K.M.C.I. [Kettle Moraine Correctional Institution]. I will accept any institutional assignment. I will successfully pass the G.E.D. [high-school-equivalency test]. I will accept any A.A. [Alcoholics Anonymous] program that may be arranged for me. I will receive no more than three minor conduct reports. I am asking to go to K.M.C.I. August 1, [1975,] then after the course, to be transferred to minimum-security status. I am asking for a release date of April 23, 1976."

A spokesman for the reformatory then says that he could guarantee the necessary arrangements.

Parole board member: I can remember talking to you in the boys' home about graduating to adult institutions. No doubt about it—you've remained unchecked. There you said you realized your drinking problem and your bad peer group; now you're here for two very serious life-threatening offenses. The judge gave you a very light sentence, probably because of your age. The problem is in believing you're sincere, because you've floated through so many institutions. The next time it might be a serious mistake to let you out, because you might kill somebody. You do not mention any treatment programs [in your proposed contract]. Why haven't you explored those?

Frankie: I did sign up to talk to the psychologist, but I didn't think to put it down [on the contract].

Board member: Is that because you didn't want [treatment]?

Frankie: No. I think it might be necessary.

Board member: You're not just saying that? You don't seem too sincere. . . . And the target release date is ridiculous. Maybe it's your youth—you're used to coming out quickly from juvenile institutions. Why did you pick a year exactly?

Frankie: My M.R. [mandatory release date] is two years and five months. I figured a year here, and then a year or two on parole. . . .

Board member: You'll have more than that on [parole]. You'll get a full four [years]. For the release date, I couldn't go along with anything less than December 17, 1976—and that's if it includes a treatment program.

Coordinator: Could we break for a few minutes?

Board member: Sure.

Frankie and the coordinator go outside the room. Five minutes later, they return.

Coordinator: Frankie is very amenable to any kind of treatment program. He would like to present some minor changes. He'd still like the alcohol program, but with a new date. He suggests going to [a correctional] camp at Winnebago in August, [1976, and] spending September and October on work-release. He's shooting for a parole on the first Wednesday in November—November 3.

Board member: You're countering with another offer. But December 17 is the minimum as far as I'm concerned. I would still think that's extremely generous in view of the past record. You've got to realize you aren't in a juvenile institution. . . .

Frankie: I think I'll take the contract, so I'll definitely know when I'm getting out.

Outside the hearing room, Frankie assesses the results of the negotiations. "I think I did fairly well. I was hoping for [parole] fifteen months from now, but I ended up with two months more [than that]. I'm still kind of lucky, since I was at the boys' school twice. I took the contract because of the definite release date. This will take one more worry off my mind."

Contract parole in Wisconsin has been known as Mutual Agreement Programming (MAP), a title used by a national project that developed the concept. Contract parole, or MAP, was first presented to corrections officials in 1972; by 1976 it was in use in nine states: Wisconsin, Maryland, Florida, Georgia, Maine, Massachusetts, Michigan, Minnesota and North Carolina.

States with MAP programs have adapted the basic model to fit their own needs and laws. For example, Maryland has combined contract parole with a voucher system for all women inmates. The state has provided offenders who sign parole contracts with up to $3,000 in vouchers to enable them to buy, largely outside the prison, educational and other services that are needed to complete contracts. In Massachusetts, officials have tied contracts to restitution for the victim of an inmate's crime: the victim has helped negotiate the parole contract, which has included a provision for restitution payments that have been set to begin when the offender is on work-release. A majority of the offenders involved committed property crimes. North Carolina's contracts have been signed by furniture manufacturers promising to hire offenders who have completed a course in furniture making.

The range of program possibilities varies considerably from state to state. Parole dates are nonnegotiable in some places; elsewhere, they are the focus of much discussion. In all the contract parole programs, inmates enter into contracts voluntarily. Those who withdraw from the program or fail to meet the contract terms revert to the regular parole process, supposedly without penalty or prejudice. In many states, contracts can be renegotiated if the inmate fails to live up to his agreement. In some states as many as half of all inmates with MAP contracts have failed to complete them, according to officials. Some states have heated personal confrontations between inmates and parole board negotiators; in other states, the contracts are developed through paperwork rather than meetings.

While contract parole has obvious advantages for inmates —a definite parole date, specific program objectives, and in some cases, the possibility of early release—proponents have felt that administrators and parole boards have benefited even more. Leon Leiberg, the man who developed MAP, has seen it as a catalyst for major reforms within state systems. "What MAP does is to force the department to begin to look at what it has [in the way of programs] and to look outside [the department] to what exists there," Leiberg says. The key is accountability: a contract forces an institution to account for the availability and the effectiveness of its programs, and it forces a parole board to define its criteria for release. In return, Leiberg says, a system can expect reduced tension in prisons, increased inmate motivation, lower costs resulting from less time served in institutions, better program coordination, fewer parole hearings, and immediate input from the parole board regarding an offender's program while he is incarcerated.

The MAP idea has not been universally popular, however. Many people have taken a "show me" attitude; a few have expressed outright opposition.

One of the most outspoken critics of MAP has been Lawrence Carpenter, regional director of the U.S. Board of Parole for the north-central region. Carpenter is the former executive director of the corrections task force of the National Advisory Commission on Criminal Justice Standards and Goals.

"Mutual Agreement Programming sounds like a good idea, but it isn't," Carpenter said. "Whenever I have seen it used, administrators have used it to impose arbitrary and senseless requirements upon offenders. . . . Also, the idea is inherently unsound. I have known prisoners who could complete almost any set of goals, but who would still be dangerous to be paroled. On the other hand, I know of prisoners who could be paroled safely without any need to meet goals. The idea is unfair to the inmates, and it is unfair to the public."

Chapter 4
Community Programs for Offenders

"How can you run a state prison system without a state prison?"

This question, posed by a prison guard in Vermont, was not rhetorical. His state has been doing just that since August 7, 1975. On that date, Vermont's only maximum-security institution, Windsor prison, built in 1809, was closed.

The key to running a correctional system without such a prison is "community corrections," Vermont believes. So, first, the offenders deemed truly dangerous—about a dozen —were transferred to the federal prison system, then the state's remaining 350 inmates were placed in small community-based facilities.

While Vermont is the only state without a state prison, it does not stand alone with regard to community corrections, which has become a national trend. Vermont's alternative facilities consist mostly of centers near the offender's own community. There the men or women progress toward extended furloughs and eventual freedom with the help of vocational training, work-release or education-release. Other states have experimented with other kinds of programs.

Corrections pioneers have come up with a number of options: halfway houses; special residential programs for alcoholics or drug addicts; work centers; restitution centers. Ex-inmates have developed some of their own programs. In addition, there has been a renewed interest in probation, which avoids any removal from society at all. Other programs are introduced frequently.

Community corrections, its proponents claim, can avoid the debilitating effects of large prisons; by avoiding incarceration in the first place, they say, the problem of reintegrating offenders is eliminated. Since an offender got into trouble in "free" society, that is the place to teach him how to behave in a socially acceptable manner. Proponents also point to the lower costs of programs that do not have to spend heavily for security.

Can Delinquents Be Saved by the Sea?

Some of the most imaginative approaches to the problem of dealing with offenders within the community were developed for juveniles. In Florida, for instance, amid palm trees and by the sea, troubled teen-agers are taught scuba diving and seamanship, and are rewarded with week-long cruises to the Bahamas. The teachers are scientists, college dropouts and adventurers. Classes are so casual that one student lounged through a mathematics lesson bare-chested, with a pet boa constrictor around his neck.

This is the atmosphere at the Florida Ocean Sciences Institute (FOSI), located at Deerfield Beach. The institute is a privately operated corrections program, funded in part by the state.

Several sister programs have also been put into operation throughout Florida. Together they form a nonprofit federation known as the Associated Marine Institutes (AMI). FOSI usually enrolls about forty youngsters. AMI officials say that most of them, under the supervision of Florida's Division of Youth Services, would have been sent to state training schools (reformatories) if FOSI did not exist.

The basic premise behind AMI is that states can use their natural resources to stimulate productive behavior in juvenile offenders. In Florida, that resource is the sea, with its challenges and glamour. In other states, officials believe, similar methods could be adapted to mountains, rivers, the desert or any other aspect of the environment.

The trainees live at home, for the most part, although a handful live in foster group homes. They attend the program eight hours a day for up to nine months. In addition to basic education classes, they are trained in seamanship, diving and other nautical skills. But the basic aims of the program are to modify behavior and teach work habits, not necessarily to train young men for the marine industry. "The sea is a vehicle, a gimmick if you like, to bring about change," says Robert Rosof, the founder and president of AMI.

Shortly after eight o'clock one morning, three white vans arrived among the palm trees at the Cove Shopping Center in Deerfield Beach. They pulled up to FOSI headquarters, a white storefront flanked by a doctor's office and a real-estate firm. Groups of tanned, long-haired teen-aged boys emerged from the vans. Some live up to forty miles away, and had been in the vans since six-thirty.

"Hey," one of them shouted. "We've got to go pick up a forty-five-foot boat. Out of sight!"

"Man, it's only a twenty-eight-footer," another youth replied.

The two youths and others soon left to get the yacht that had been donated to FOSI. This was the day's seamanship class. Trainees would carefully check out the boat. Then, under the instructor's supervision, they would maneuver it to a marina near the shopping center where FOSI maintains a small boat-repair yard.

On a normal day another vanload of kids would be heading for classes at the county adult education center. But this day, as a reward for good work at the center, they were being taken to the Everglades for a ride in a boat that skims atop the water. Another group of nine youths was at sea, on a week-long training cruise through the Florida Keys, aboard the forty-one-foot *FOSI II*.

The remainder of FOSI's forty-or-so trainees were attending classes in the storefront, a former grocery store. It resembled a diving-equipment shop. Black rubber scuba suits, plankton-collecting devices and other sea gear drape the partitions. On one wall was a bank of nine small aquariums aswarm with tropical fish.

In one room, its walls covered with navigation charts, seven youths were studying lifesaving and water safety. A tattooed youth wearing a black T-shirt cut off at the shoulders was slouched at a table, reading a waterproof edition of the "Fishwatcher's Guide" that can be taken on dives. The instructor, Randy Wilkins, with sun-bleached hair and wearing sunglasses, was perched cross-legged on an old desk in the corner.

"When do I get my aquarium?" a boy asked.

"Later today," Wilkins said. "Some guys haven't been doing a good job, so you'll get one of theirs."

The boy must sign a contract agreeing to collect shells, stones and live specimens for the tank, and must maintain it. In return, FOSI will provide him with diving gear and send him on field trips where he can collect the specimens.

The major incentive for all the boys in the class is the chance to earn official certification as scuba divers. To achieve this, they must study a series of manuals and learn some math and physics essential to diving.

To enter an institute, a youth must be between the ages of fifteen and eighteen. He must have at least average intelligence, and sixth-grade abilities in reading and math. And the courts or the Division of Youth Services must refer him there. He doesn't have to love the water, but he mustn't be afraid of it. The institutes refuse to accept youths who have repeatedly been involved with drugs or exhibited assaultive behavior. "We can't work with the hard-core twenty percent," says FOSI's program director, Kerry Clemmons. "We admit it."

The prospective trainee is given educational and psychological tests, and a swimming test. If the examinations show there is a chance he will succeed, he is enrolled in a thirty-day trial and examination period.

"Right away he's issued a diving mask, fins and snorkel," says Ed Henderson, an AMI administrative assistant. "We tell him if he completes the program, they're his to keep. We show him slides of cruises and other activities, to hang a carrot in front of him. We try to teach kids that if they do good things, good things will happen to them."

When a youth is accepted, he and the institute draw up a contract. It sets individual goals for the training period, scaled to realistic expectations for achievement in a dozen categories, including diving, seamanship, lifesaving, ocean science, first aid, electives such as photography and marine maintenance, plus family relationships and behavior. The minimum training period is six months. After that, the trainee can elect to specialize for three additional months in one of the marine trades.

One apparent success at FOSI was Ed Wood. Formerly a heroin addict who had stolen repeatedly to finance his habit, Ed Wood left FOSI a hero. One day he and a buddy were practicing boat maneuvers at the marina when they saw a small private plane crash a few hundred yards away. They raced the boat to the scene, put out the flames and pulled the pilot from the cockpit. For their action they received a presidential commendation.

"I changed a lot here," Wood said in an interview. "I settled down and learned a lot about responsibility. Many of us, no one had ever given responsibility to. Here, when you go diving you're responsible for your buddy's life."

A Refuge from Gang Wars

Community programs don't have to have palm trees and yachts. One program operates in a very different type of environment—a neighborhood that is among the toughest in Philadelphia. When it began in 1969, the program focused on youngsters involved in gang warfare. Its method: to inspire intense family feelings within a framework of African-inspired black consciousness. Its name: the House of Umoja.

Umoja is the Swahili word for "unity." The House of Umoja began as a publishing venture. In 1969, however, a series of letters to a magazine it was publishing led Sister Falaka Fattah, the woman who runs the House of Umoja, to look into the youth gang problem. That year was dubbed "the year of the gun" by the Philadelphia media because of gang violence.

Sister Falaka's husband, Daoud, who had been a gang member himself, returned to the street for three months to study the gangs while Sister Falaka began to see possible solutions to the violence, she says, in "the strength of the family, tribal concepts and African value systems."

Sister Falaka said it made sense to her to try and re-create an African-style extended family where members of the gangs could find alternative values to their street-life culture. One reason it made sense was that she and her husband had six sons of their own, a ready-made framework for an extended family.

In 1969 the couple invited fifteen boys, members of Philadelphia's Clymer Street gang, to come and live with them.
Of this original group, Sister Falaka said, seven went to
college, seven got regular jobs and one went to jail. She
maintained that some members of the Clymer Street gang
who did not come to the House of Umoja are now among
the leaders of organized black crime in Philadelphia.

In its first five years the House of Umoja sheltered more
than three hundred youngsters. They belonged to seventy-
three different street gangs. On the street, members of two
rival gangs would fight over who had stepped on the wrong
bit of sidewalk. In the House, members of the same two
gangs shared bedrooms. Of the first three hundred residents,
only ten were arrested since leaving the House, as far as
Sister Falaka knows.

The House of Umoja has owned twenty houses on one
block of Frazier Street in West Philadelphia. Although the
property lay on the turf of the Moon gang, agreement was
reached among gangs from all parts of the city that the
House of Umoja and its properties be neutral territory. No
one living there was to be harmed. The House served as a
crisis intervention center to help avoid gang wars and to try
to prevent killings if quarrels did erupt.

Sister Falaka bases her formula on the perception that
a street gang provides the same emotional and material
security for its members that an extended family does. The
House of Umoja tried to do the same thing, but it forbade
destructive behavior. "The House of Umoja is not about
breaking up gangs," Sister Falaka said. "It's about stopping
killing."

But the House also makes sure its members know how to
fight with their hands so they can control any battles that
threaten the family. One broke out at a House-sponsored
conference, and twenty Umoja members "handled" it, Sister Falaka said. The House also teaches members to recog-

nize other kinds of gangs—what Sister Falaka called "the gang in city hall and the gang in Washington that pulled off Watergate."

All the brothers, as members of the House are always called, earn money from odd jobs for carfare, pocket money and nominal House dues. Cash prizes are also awarded to brothers who display special knowledge about things. "That's how it is on the outside," said Sister Falaka. "The more you know and the more you do, the more you're supposed to get paid in our society."

Something more important than money in the House of Umoja, however, are the African names that the brothers earn—for their efforts to master the House's philosophy, for the help they give one another, for the work they do to improve the House and for what they do in the community. Brothers must earn an African first name, and then they go through seven stages to earn full membership in the extended family. At that point they are given the family name, Fattah. Staff members as well as brothers can earn this name.

The House of Umoja organizes activities on a seasonal rather than a monthly schedule. Sister Falaka said this is another feature of the House which is of African origin. The brothers are expected to relate seasonal concepts—birth in spring, marriage in summer, children in fall, and death in winter—to their own lives. At the end of winter in mid-March, for example, the brothers were discussing senseless death and death for a cause, using Martin Luther King, Jr., as an example of the latter. The timing of activities also is related to nature, with the brothers getting up at 6 A.M., when the sun usually rises, rather than at 3 or 4 P.M., which is the normal rising hour for youngsters who are on the street.

The brothers attend classes in the African component of

their program at the House. They go to regular Philadelphia schools for academic or vocational education. One group of brothers included seven students at a Philadelphia community college, all of whom had earned their high-school-equivalency certificates while living at the House.

Sister Falaka does not think it would be easy to replicate the House of Umoja in other cities, but she said it was not impossible. She said that if two brothers from another city lived in the House for several months, and then went back and took some brothers with them, particularly those who have earned their Fattah names, it might work. "But we cannot write down a manual," she said. "The house is a family, not a social agency. It was started by a husband and wife and their six sons. It needs that blood family."

Restitution

Many corrections officials believe that property offenders—those convicted of crimes such as burglary or forgery—do not usually require the tight security of a prison. But often they are sent to prison because there is no alternative.

Roy Olson (not his real name) was a property offender. He occupied a cell, which he was nervously pacing, at the Minnesota State Prison at Stillwater. He was serving a five-year sentence for burglary, having broken into the home of a St. Paul minister.

In half an hour he would meet that minister in prison.

The Reverend Jerome G. Bangert and his wife were also uncomfortable as they sat in the visiting room of the prison waiting for Olson to appear. The burglary and its aftermath had been a painful experience, especially for Mrs. Bangert. She and her husband were not particularly anxious to meet Roy Olson.

The meeting was tense. Olson was so nervous and

ashamed that he could hardly talk. "I felt awful cheap and low because they were such nice people," he recalled later. "I feel funny yet. . . ."

To make Roy Olson "feel funny" about what he had done was one of the purposes of the meeting. The other purpose was to help him get out of prison so he could pay back the Bangerts. The meeting had been set up by the Minnesota Restitution Center, founded in 1972. The center's guiding principle is that criminals should pay for their crimes by working and paying back their victims, not by sitting in a prison cell.

Minnesota corrections officials say the primary advantage of the restitution center is that it finally focuses attention on the victim of crime, whom the criminal-justice system has long neglected. Other community corrections programs across the country have picked up the idea and are now making restitution a key element of their treatment units.

Officials say that the center also saves the state what they consider the extravagant expense of keeping nondangerous property offenders locked up. Not long ago it cost the taxpayers between $16 and $25 a day to keep an offender in a Minnesota prison. Restitution center officials estimated their cost at $14.50 a day. And, they pointed out, the men in the center are paying taxes, supporting families who might otherwise be on welfare, and of course, paying back their victims.

Roy Olson was caught in the act of burglarizing Rev. Bangert's house, so Olson gained nothing from the crime. He ended up paying $120 in restitution to cover the loss of the couple's time in court and the cost of several visits to the doctor by Mrs. Bangert, who, her husband said, was "very upset" by the incident.

The meetings between the offenders and their victims have all the elements of high drama. Both become more aware of the human side of crime and punishment. The meetings can be a startling experience for the offender, who generally has never had to face one of his victims, as well as for the victim, who generally has never had a conversation with a criminal nor seen the inside of a prison.

Rev. Bangert, for instance, said that before he met Roy Olson he envisioned Olson and other criminals as snarling, vindictive creatures straight out of a television police series. Instead, Olson turned out to be very human and very apologetic. He explained to Rev. Bangert that he had been drunk when he committed the crime and had not meant to hurt anybody.

Before he met Olson, Rev. Bangert said he was "happy [Olson] was caught and locked up." After meeting him, the clergyman said he was "very anxious for him to get out of there. . . . Out of the whole thing, the thing that has amazed me the most is that I had the impression for so many years that something was being done for these people. [But] I couldn't see where Stillwater was going to do much for this type of person."

Olson had a criminal history dating back twenty-five years. Asked whether he had ever before thought about the victims of his crimes, he replied, "No, never." He said the experience affected him profoundly.

In Olson's case, when the judge sent him to prison for the burglary, he had only been free for a few months after serving three years for grand larceny. He had served another previous term in a Wisconsin prison and numerous county jail terms. This time, in the Bangert case, he expected to serve his entire five-year sentence before being set free. Instead, his name was picked by a computer at the University of Minnesota as a candidate for the restitution center. To his utter astonishment, the Minnesota Corrections Authority—the state paroling agency—paroled him after only four months in prison to the center's austere quarters on the seventh floor of the Minneapolis YMCA.

Olson joined about twenty other offenders also chosen at random to be paroled to the center. All, like Olson, had been released after only four months; most of them would normally have spent at least two years in jail. Before they are released from prison, they must sign a contract in which they agree to abide by the rules of the center, to get and hold a job, and to use part of their earnings to make regular payments to their victims. They must also agree to pay $12.50 a week for room and board, and to participate in center and outside therapy programs if they have psychiatric, alcohol or drug problems. If they successfully complete the program, they are released to regular parole supervision, which normally lasts until the expiration date of their original sentence.

The restitution center includes a wide variety of treatment programs, ranging from a multi-step behavior modification plan to Synanon-type attack therapy. Many residents have clauses in their contracts—often at the insistence of the parole board—requiring that they join Alcoholics Anonymous or seek drug counseling.

Center residents proceed through four phases. With each phase they acquire more personal freedom, such as the right to stay in their own homes overnight or on weekends. Phase IV is release from the center to regular parole supervision. Offenders do not need to complete their restitution contracts while living in the center; most contracts involving the repayment of large sums are completed while the offender is on the street.

But the face-to-face interaction between the victim and the offender is "one of the original concepts that really hasn't panned out well," Center Director Robert Mowatt says. To start with, he explains, a surprisingly large number of victims wanted nothing to do with the offender or the center—and didn't even want their money back. Others agreed to sign the restitution contract but did not want to travel to the prison to meet the offender, often saying that they could not take off from work. Many contracts have been negotiated by third parties, usually the center's parole counselors. Once the offender has been released from prison to the center, he is encouraged, but not obligated, to make the first payment in person. Even if he does make one payment personally, the practice now is to send the rest through the mail.

In the first three years of the program, some one hundred offenders repaid $16,000 to their victims.

Ex-Offender Programs

While corrections officials have developed some alternatives to prison, other innovative programs have come from former inmates. Their approach to the offender is often unexpectedly "hard." Take John Maher, for example. He thinks that drug addicts are "bums"—human parasites who generally have lost any vestige of integrity. They will betray their best friends to obtain drugs. They will steal from their own mothers to keep the hypodermic needle full. They are "pathetic" human specimens who make a life style of lying and cheating. They often leave a trail of abandoned wives and children in their endless pursuit of heroin, or end up selling their wives and daughters into prostitution to support their insatiable habits. They are whining, impulsive "children," Maher says, who want instant gratification of their every whim, but have generally never done a full day's work in their lives.

As evidence, Maher offers himself. He learned about heroin at the age of twelve, and spent the next ten years supporting his habit through burglary, shoplifting, procuring, drug pushing and numbers running in his native New York City. His only aspiration in life was to become a small-time gangster.

83

Now in his mid-thirties, John Maher lives in a thirty-room baronial mansion on posh Pacific Heights in San Francisco. He got there not by pursuing his underworld career, but by switching sides and becoming a self-proclaimed social reformer.

Maher is now the law-abiding president, chairman of the board, resident guru and tribal chieftain of the Delancey Street Foundation, an organization founded on his belief that the human wreckage manufactured by the drug culture is salvageable. Since he founded Delancey Street about five years ago, Maher claims to have developed a method of converting drug addicts and other ex-offenders from "bums" into hard-working restaurant workers, moving men, construction workers, businessmen, salesmen and generally useful citizens. What's more, he maintains, he did it without financial help from the federal government or foundations, and without the cadre of psychiatrists, psychologists, social workers, counselors and "creep consultants," as he calls them, who "come out of the woodwork" to dominate most other projects.

Delancey Street has been operated almost entirely by about 270 ex-addicts, many of whom were also thieves, burglars and armed robbers. Its members (a conglomerate of blacks, whites, Chicanos and Puerto Ricans from all over the country) range in age from eight to fifty-eight and consider themselves a "family." The family once resided not in an abandoned building in the low-income district of San Francisco, but in the former Egyptian consulate in Pacific Heights, one of the nation's most exclusive neighborhoods, and in the former Russian consulate, two blocks away. They had to give up the former when the Egyptians wanted to move in again, but they remain in the latter, and maintain other residences, too.

The Delancey Street family runs on a communal economy. Its main sources of income are donations and profits

Minnesota Prison Ombudsman Theartrice Williams (right) talks to an inmate at Stillwater Prison.

◀ Door to a cell at Trenton (N.J.) State Prison, constructed in 1836. Although intended for use by one inmate, such cells have housed three to four men.

A guard at Trenton (N.J.) State Prison lowers a key to the main door so that supplies can be brought into the facility.

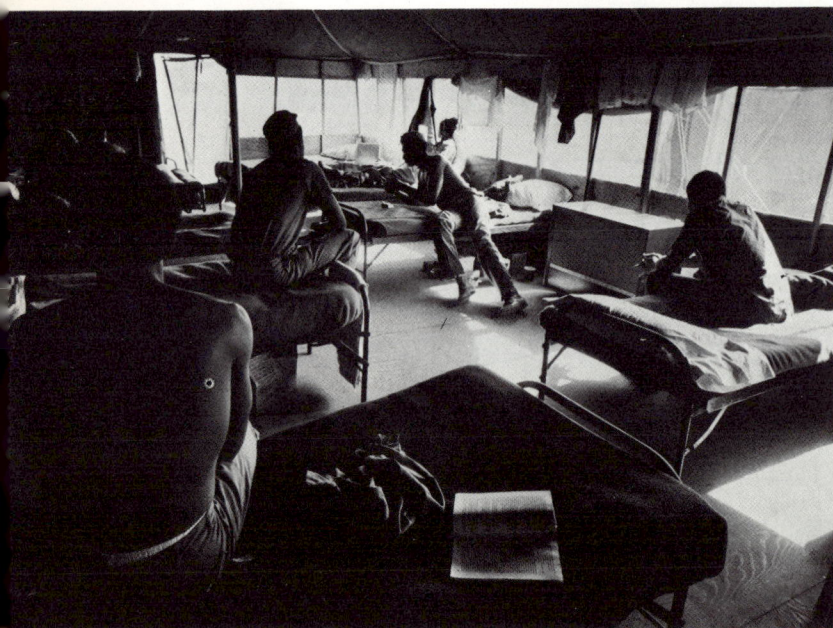

Top: Due to overcrowding, inmates have lived in tents at the Florida State Prison in Starkey.

Bottom: Inmates relax in one of the tents at Starkey.

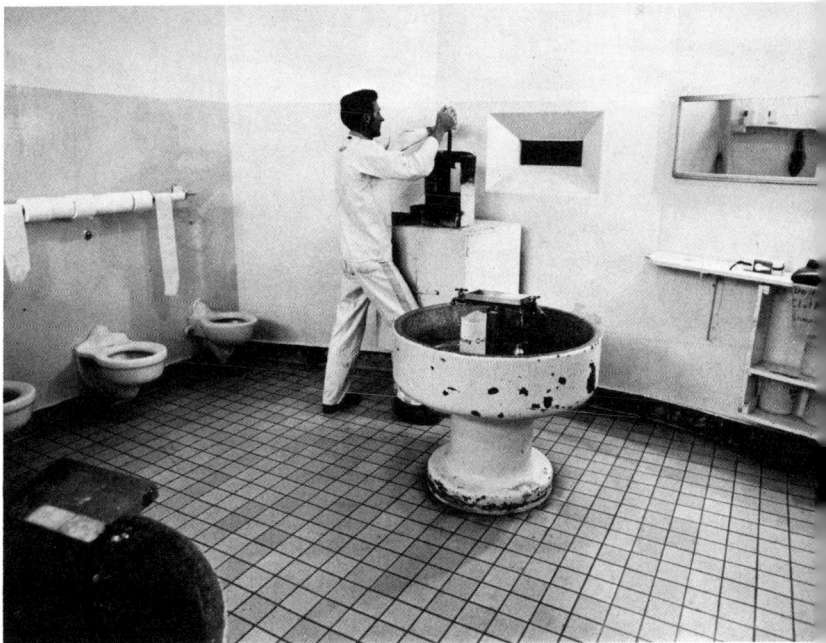

Top: A dining hall at San Quentin Prison in California. In the background is a mural depicting state history.

Bottom: An inmate at Reidsville State Prison in Georgia works on a leather-embossing machine located in a lavatory.

A Georgia inmate operates a metal-cutting machine in the Reidsville State Prison license-plate factory.

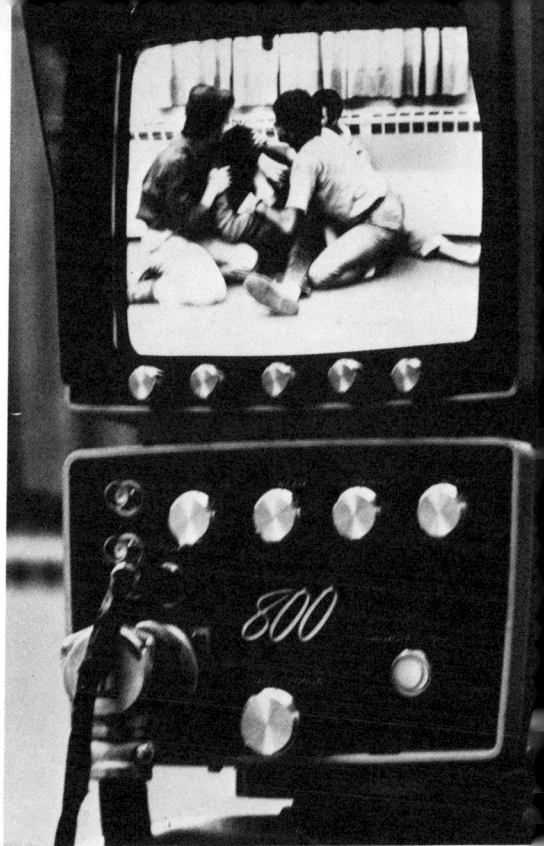

Top: A sex offender treatment program in New Jersey video-tapes a simulated therapy session.

Bottom: Inmates in the main exercise yard at Trenton (N.J.) State Prison.

A youth at the Worcester (Mass.) Intensive Care Unit, a locked facility for juveniles in trouble with the law.

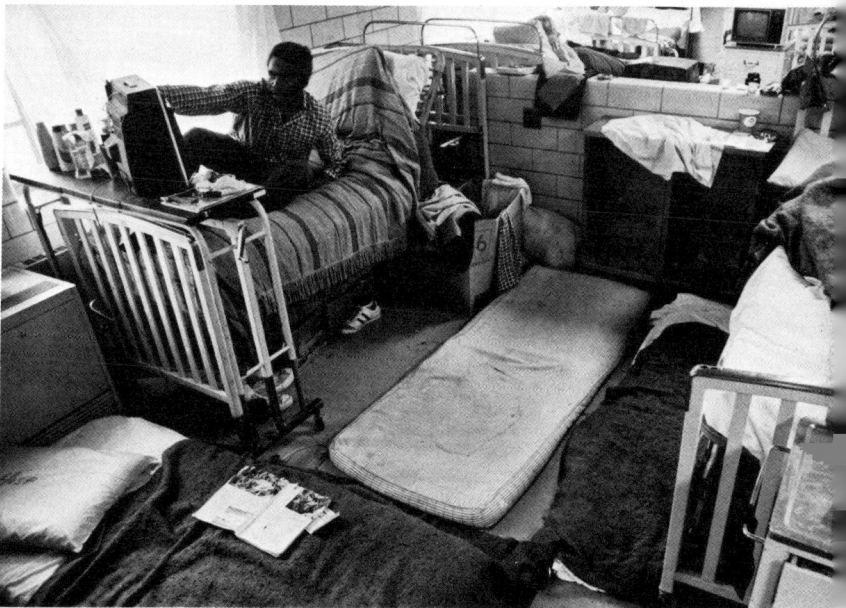

Top: A resident decorates his room at Hastings House, a group home for juveniles in Cambridge, Mass.

Bottom: Overcrowding at Concord Prison in Massachusetts forced some inmates who were not patients to sleep on mattresses on the floor of the prison hospital.

Top: A member of the Minnesota prison ombudsman's staff (facing camera) talks with an inmate.

Bottom: Inmates at Stillwater Prison, Minn., can leave messages for the ombudsman and for other prison officials in specially designated mailboxes.

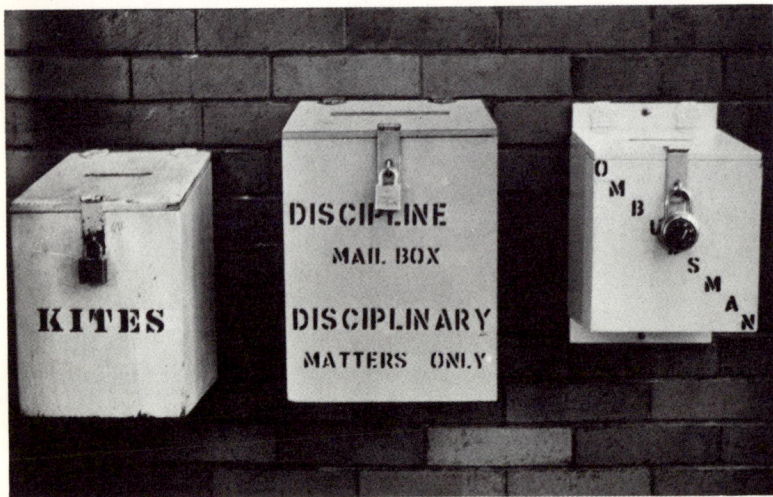

Opposite page: Inmate Peter Makarewicz, who was sentenced in Massachusetts to a life term for first-degree murder, leaves Walpole Prison on the start of a twelve-hour furlough.

Top: While on furlough, Makarewicz tries on a sports jacket at a local shop.

Bottom: Makarewicz and his mother enjoy breakfast in the backyard of her house.

Makarewicz is thoroughly searched upon his return to Walpole. His life sentence has been commuted, but he must serve additional time on an attempted escape charge and expects to be released next year.

The privately operated Florida Ocean Sciences Institute (FOSI) believes that states can use their natural resources to stimulate productive behavior in juvenile offenders. Most of the youths who come to FOSI have been in trouble with the law and are trying to overcome their problems in activities that include scuba diving and sailing.

PHOTOS BY BILL POWERS FOR *CORRECTIONS* MAGAZINE

Top: The Delancey Street Foundation in San Francisco helps ex-offenders with therapy sessions and with jobs in businesses that include a Delancey Street Restaurant.

Bottom: An interior view of the Delancey Street Restaurant.

Two youths at Camp Hill, a maximum-security unit for juveniles in Pennsylvania. Dr. Jerome Miller, State Commissioner for Youth, is attempting to close the unit. ▶

from a group of family-owned businesses; it is thus largely self-sufficient. The organization keeps all its members adequately fed, clothed and housed, and provides work, vocational training and schooling.

Delancey Street's treatment program is based on the proposition that the best people to rehabilitate drug addicts and criminals are other drug addicts and criminals. The most effective treatment, Delancey Street's leaders believe, is hard work in the family residences and businesses, combined with frequent, brutal "attack therapy" sessions.

Maher was rescued from drug addiction by his participation in Synanon, a California-based community of drug addicts. Over a period of eight years he rose to a position of importance in Synanon. Then, in 1970, Maher moved out on his own. His prescription for the rehabilitation of drug addicts was simple: "We did something very radical. We went to work for a living."

According to Maher, he started Delancey Street with a $1,000 gift from an underworld loan shark. At one point his family of ex-addicts had a gross annual income of more than $500,000, he claims. The money was generated through raffles, donations and five family-owned businesses: a restaurant, a garage, a flower and terrarium business, a moving company, and a construction and building-maintenance business. Delancey Street's income has always covered most expenses, with small deficits made up through donations.

Maher believes in the up-by-the-bootstraps American dream. He chose the name Delancey Street because of his admiration for the hard work and ethnic unity that helped many immigrants emerge from poverty. Many of those immigrants poured off the boats at the turn of the century onto Delancey Street, in Lower Manhattan.

No one, including Maher, draws any salary, either for work done at the residences or in the businesses. The no-salary rule has a practical basis. It renders all family members

85

equally penniless, making them totally dependent on Delancey Street for their every need, and preventing quarrels over money. More important, if family members were paid even token salaries, the family businesses, and Delancey Street as a whole, would long ago have gone bankrupt.

In addition to agreeing to work for no salary, newcomers to Delancey Street must take a "vow of poverty" before being admitted, giving up all their worldly goods to Delancey Street.

The surrender of their property is only one in a succession of deprivations that newcomers to Delancey Street must undergo. If a male newcomer agrees to accept all the rules, he is immediately taken to the basement to have his head shaved.

Some people come to Delancey Street on their own for help, but the courts refer many others. Delancey Street members go over the dockets of the local criminal and juvenile courts in search of likely candidates. The project goes to great lengths to maintain good relationships with judges, probation officers and parole agents.

There are five basic rules for family members:

- No "chemicals," including drugs and alcohol.
- No physical violence.
- Everyone must work or go to school. (Those who go to school also work.)
- No "promiscuity." ("Trial marriages" are permitted, but they must be officially approved and quasi-permanent.)
- A commitment of two years.

Hard work is only one of the pillars upon which Delancey Street rests. The other is the "games"—subtly structured sessions of "attack therapy." These are used to keep resentment and hostility from building, and also to explore inner feelings.

The game begins when one player "puts the game on" another and lets loose with a series of shrill "indictments" —accusations. When the first accuser is finished, the other players may continue to pile on other indictments. The first rule for the accused is to counterattack, whether his position is justified or not. He must react, and react strongly, or he is not playing the game. If he allows himself to be bullied or beaten down, if he withdraws into himself under the attack of his peers, then the purpose of the game is defeated —that purpose being to make him angry, to draw him out emotionally and make him reveal himself.

The range of acts and attitudes that constitute unacceptable behavior are closely defined. Family members are required to display unwavering and undiluted loyalty to Delancey Street, which means loyalty to the institution, to John Maher and to other family members. This principle was illustrated during a game attended by most of Delancey Street's top brass.

The game began with a furious attack on a black game player, who was about to be trial-married to a white family member. He was accused of submitting an outrageous requisition request in preparation for his trial marriage, asking for a private room complete with bedroom furniture. How did he dare to do that when he knew that many other Delancey Street couples were at that moment without the beds and lamps and bureaus he was requesting, one player asked angrily. Furthermore, he was told, this was only the latest in a series of incidents that revealed him to be selfish and acquisitive; he was obviously ignoring the group and concentrating on keeping himself comfortable. The subject changed, and suddenly the man was being accused of standing outside the Delancey Street restaurant while his white girl friend was inside eating dinner with relatives. He was ashamed of being black, someone shouted, and suddenly a white man across the room was screaming that he was nothing but a "nigger," ashamed of the color of his skin. By this time the black man was exploding with rage; barely able to stay seated, he was screaming every obscene insult he could think of at his accusers.

Suddenly the game was "on" the black man's girl friend, who was deliberately included among the players. The man who called her boyfriend a "nigger" was screaming that she was just using him, that she didn't really want to sleep with him; she wanted him to spit-shine her shoes. Why didn't she introduce her boyfriend to her relatives? Why was she ashamed of him? She responded in a frustrated shriek that her relatives were old and wouldn't understand. The subject expanded. Why was she constantly accepting visits and presents from her parents and grandparents? Where was her allegiance, to her family or to Delancey Street? With both, she responded, but she was shouted down by a chorus of voices telling her that it could not be that way; that she would have to decide between them. She finally agreed that she was guilty of the sin of divided loyalty and promised to try to work it out somehow.

The group eventually turned on each of its members, and when the game was over, the players left together and had coffee as if nothing had happened.

This detachment of what goes on in the games from the rest of life at Delancey Street is important, the players said, and is one of the first things a new player must learn. There is always, in a properly played game, the implicit understanding that the attackers do not necessarily mean what they say, and that all personal insults are merely a vehicle for arousing emotion in the accused. The most virulent attacks usually are followed by some more calmly delivered advice. For example, the attack on both members of the interracial couple in the previously described game was followed by a more polite discussion of the handicaps they would have to overcome were they ever to leave Delancey Street and re-enter society together.

Opposition

"Community corrections is always very acceptable to the public—until you put an address on it." In this comment, Ward Murphy, director of Maine's Bureau of Corrections, sums up what many administrators have learned from bitter experience: people do not want convicted offenders for neighbors, no matter what the circumstances.

Most of the programs described in this chapter have aroused local opposition. Some of the people near Delancey Street, for example, have protested that the operation is not appropriate for their exclusive neighborhood.

Sometimes the opposition can be enough to prevent a community-oriented program from opening. In other cases, officials must plead with local residents and promise special conditions to ensure the safety of citizens. These conditions are taken seriously by the local community.

In 1969 the townspeople of St. Albans, Vermont, were told that they had nothing to fear. The modern-looking building under construction just outside of town would not be a prison; it was to be an intensive diagnostic and treatment center. It was not for hardened criminals, but for young offenders who were thought to be better off kept away from more dangerous inmates at Windsor, 133 miles away.

"We were promised everything," complained former St. Albans Alderman Stanley Cummings in the Burlington *Free Press*. "'First-time offenders only,' they told us. 'There won't be any hard-nosed criminals in there,' they said."

St. Albans, which since has been remodeled to receive inmates from Windsor, was designed originally as a "therapeutic community" where older counselors would work with

89

up to twenty first offenders who were between sixteen and twenty-seven years old. It also had twenty spaces for young offenders over fifteen who were undergoing pre-sentence evaluations.

With the closing of Windsor, St. Albans has become the most security-conscious institution in the state. St. Albans is still officially designated as a medium-security prison, but maximum-security cells for some twenty inmates have been constructed. A new dormitory-style honor wing (originally designed for youthful offenders), with individual rooms for forty inmates, has housed several of the inmates transferred from Windsor.

Meanwhile St. Albans' role as a diagnostic center has been de-emphasized. The diagnostic unit has space for only eleven inmates at a time, compared to the original twenty.

What happened to the original concept of treating only youthful first offenders? "I'm afraid it was a rather naïve idea," Corrections Commissioner Kent Stoneman says, adding that St. Albans was built without the benefit of a thorough study to see if it really was needed. "Like many other small departments of corrections around the country, this department in the past has made important decisions without knowing very much about its clientele," he says. As it turned out, many youthful first offenders were being placed on probation by the courts, not sentenced to institutions. So St. Albans, almost from the beginning, received youthful offenders who were guilty of serious offenses. In 1972 the state legislature repealed the maximum age limit of twenty-seven for inmates at St. Albans. As the role of the facility began to change, local citizens protested that the promises made in 1969 were not being kept. "I'm sorry some people see it that way," Stoneman says. "The changes had to be made."

Probation

Probation is the nation's oldest alternative to incarceration, and the most extensively used. Our probationary system can be traced to 1841; a Boston bootmaker named John Augustus became the first probation officer when he volunteered to help a man whom the judge was about to send to prison.

Probation is used most commonly for first offenders. It offers supervision and counseling in the community rather than imprisonment. Today, despite the innovative programs described earlier in this chapter, probation remains the bedrock on which any community-oriented system is based. In some states, two thirds or more of those who are convicted are placed on probation.

Many probation departments are under the supervision of counties, or even individual judges; this makes exact figures hard to come by. However, most observers agree that probation has fallen far short of its goals. Probation officers are often swamped by enormous caseloads, sometimes as high as two hundred cases per officer. They also often prepare background reports for judges on individuals prior to sentencing. The result has been in many cases that probation officers can barely keep in touch with those under their supervision, much less offer any effective monitoring or counseling. In New Jersey, for example, a court official said that a probationer was lucky if he saw his probation officer for fifteen minutes a month. A New York City probation administrator said that high caseloads meant that his officers were "shuffling paper" and "playing games" in lieu of personal contact.

In 1966 California embarked on an ambitious program to upgrade probation. Called "probation subsidy," it has been the object of great controversy in political and correctional circles for years.

California's county probation departments, like those in most urban states, were plagued for many years with caseloads so heavy that effective supervision was impossible. The state decided to zero in on this problem. From 1966 through 1974, under the probation subsidy program, the state provided the counties with $105 million in subsidies specifically earmarked to establish and maintain smaller probation caseloads for selected, hard-to-handle adult and juvenile offenders.

The Youth Authority, which is also responsible for setting standards for the smaller caseloads, administers the program. They may number no more than fifty; the average size has been twenty-eight. Conventional caseloads have been averaging seventy-five for juveniles and over a hundred for adults. Officers in charge of the smaller, subsidized caseloads must offer more than conventional supervision. The special services may include job, family, drug and other kinds of counseling, or innovative treatment such as encounter therapy, Guided Group Interaction or transactional analysis. The officer may provide these services himself or, as usually happens, contract with private agencies to provide them. The private agencies might include out-patient or residential drug-treatment centers, mental-health clinics, halfway houses and ex-offender employment programs. The salaries and training of the more than six hundred probation officers handling probation subsidy caseloads and the cost of contracting for services are the program's two major expenses.

During probation subsidy's first year of operation, when the counties had to underwrite the cost of the program in anticipation of year-end reimbursement by the state, only a few hundred offenders benefited. A few years later, there were more than 17,000 men, women, and children in special probation subsidy caseloads.

Supporters of probation subsidy hail it as the greatest reform of the criminal-justice system in the history of California. The program's critics, while acknowledging its huge impact, charge that judges and probation officers have used probation subsidy to overload the county jail system with felons, and release thousands of dangerous criminals who should be behind bars.

The program works as follows:

An offender is convicted. The county probation department prepares a pre-sentence report, which includes a recommendation for imprisonment, immediate probation or deferred probation. The last is an unusual sentencing option widely used in California, under which a judge may sentence an offender to a short county jail term as a condition of probation. Since the probation subsidy law was passed, probation officers have recommended immediate or deferred probation more often, with the knowledge that the more difficult probationers can be placed in smaller, subsidized caseloads.

No judge ever places an offender in a probation subsidy caseload; he merely places a man on probation, and it is up to probation officials to determine whether a particular offender gets special treatment. It is therefore impossible to know, without some record of each judge's thinking in each case, whether an individual offender has been spared prison because of a judge's confidence in probation subsidy, or whether the offender is a beneficiary of a general tendency among judges across the nation to award probation more liberally in recent years.

Although the architects of the original law did not foresee it, probation subsidy caused immediate, drastic cuts in the state's prison population. In 1964 there were 30,000 inmates in the adult prison system, and the number of yearly commitments to the Department of Corrections was at an all-time high—about 6,000 per year. Based on rising crime and

93

conviction rates, officials predicted that the prison population would double in a decade.

But by fiscal 1968–69, probation subsidy's third year of operation, commitments to the adult prisons had dropped to 3,830—the lowest number since 1955. It has been estimated that as many as 40,000 offenders were kept out of the state prison system by probation subsidy between 1966 and 1974.

Why did probation subsidy have such an impact? The major reason was the incentive for counties to send fewer people to prison.

The officials who wrote the probation subsidy law decided that the state should do more than simply give the counties money to improve probation services. They concluded they must also tie the awarding of state subsidies to a reduction by the counties in the rate of commitments to the state correctional system. If the reduction in commitments was large enough, they reasoned, the saving to the state of the cost of incarceration would more than offset the amount of the subsidy. Thus was born the "performance factor," the most controversial aspect of probation subsidy.

The law that was finally adopted stipulates that no county will receive a state subsidy unless it performs—that is, unless it reduces the rate of commitments to the state. To qualify for a state subsidy, a county must improve upon its average rate of commitment per 100,000 population for the years 1959 through 1963. If the county succeeds in reducing its commitments below this "base" rate, it will receive from the state $2,080 to $4,000 for every offender it has placed on probation and not sent to the state prison system. Each county's subsidy is computed annually.

In recent years a series of attempts have been made to substantially modify or even eliminate the probation subsidy program. Spearheaded by law-enforcement officials and their allies in the legislative and executive branches of the state government, the opposition campaign has been led by Los Angeles Police Chief Ed Davis, who denounced probation subsidy as an "insidious" abuse of judicial discretion, in which the state pays "blood money" to the counties to keep armed robbers and murderers at large. Davis charged that his officers are constantly arresting offenders, especially juveniles, who have been released because of probation subsidy.

The concept of probation subsidy received a blow in 1975. In a report to the state legislature, a study group found no difference in recidivism between offenders placed in special caseloads and those sent to institutions and then released on parole. Neither was there any difference between those in the special caseloads of about thirty offenders per officer and those in the regular probation caseloads, which number from seventy-five to more than a hundred.

One-to-One Counseling

Even thirty people is far too many for any one officer to get to know, say some defenders of probation. It has often been suggested that it would cost a state less to hire a full-time supervisor for each offender than to send that offender to prison. A private program for juveniles in Massachusetts has tried to approach that goal. One of its cases dealt with a boy we will call Joey.

Joey was twelve years old. He was a thin, frail-looking youngster, well under five feet tall. He was very shy and didn't talk much.

Joey lived in the Great Brook Valley public housing project, a sprawling collection of one-story cinderblock buildings in the north end of Worcester, Massachusetts. He had twenty-one brothers and sisters, though only six of them still lived in the project. Joey's mother, a nervous, emaciated woman, wasn't much bigger than he. She was a conscientious mother, rising early every day to wash, clean and cook.

95

But she often found it difficult to control her children, most of whom were in foster homes.

When he was ten, Joey, more for entertainment than personal gain, began stealing cars. He and his friends from the project reportedly stole twenty to twenty-five cars in the course of two years, specializing in Lincoln Continentals. Once they tried to steal an airplane.

Joey was caught several times and placed on probation, but it did no good, and an exasperated judge finally committed him to the state Department of Youth Services (DYS). At one time, commitment would have meant a stay at a state training school. But those institutions are closed now (Massachusetts shut all its major juvenile institutions in 1971), and DYS has had to find more innovative ways of dealing with delinquents like Joey. The guiding principle is to do everything possible to keep them in their own homes, especially those as young as Joey.

Joey was placed in the care of the Community Advancement Program (CAP), Massachusetts' largest and, some say, most effective nonresidential treatment and supervision program. As a result, Joey never had to leave home.

Youngsters in CAP are placed in the care of counselors with caseloads of no more than five, and sometimes as few as two. The counselors' most important responsibility is to know where the youths are and what they are doing twenty-four hours a day, seven days a week. They have to see each of their charges four or more times a week. They are responsible for keeping them employed or in school, for their recreation, for vocational and educational counseling, for seeing that they get proper medical and dental care. If a youth gets into new trouble with the law, the counselors intervene on his behalf with the police and courts. If he has problems at school, the counselor tries to work it out with the teacher. He is expected to make frequent visits to the youth's home and talks about his progress with his parents. He often ends up being counselor not only to the child but also to his parents, brothers, sisters and friends.

CAP's treatment program has three components: "tracking," regular or "outreach" supervision, and foster care. Because he had to be watched almost all the time to keep him out of trouble, Joey was assigned to tracking.

"Tracking was instituted because DYS said the price of residential care was too high," says Bill Wolfe, president of CAP. "They said they would rather keep a [seriously delinquent] kid in a nonresidential setting, at his own home, if we could guarantee that we would know what the kid was doing. So I wrote up a proposal for tracking. And that's what we do. We track kids. We shadow kids. We're on their backs, we're in their hair. We know where they are and what they're doing all the time. A counselor never has more than two or three tracking kids."

CAP's contract with DYS guarantees that each tracking youth will have at least five hours of supervision a day, seven days a week, and that his counselor or other staff members will be on call twenty-four hours a day for crisis invervention. For this service, DYS pays CAP $97 a week per child— about half what it would cost to hold him in a group home, or in one of the old institutions. Youngsters in the regular program get a minimum of fifteen hours a week supervision, at a cost to DYS of $63 a week.

CAP counselors carry both regular and tracking kids in their caseloads. Youngsters in the regular program who become difficult to manage can be moved into the tracking program, with DYS approval, and those in tracking can be moved down into the regular program.

Youths in both programs are encouraged, but not required, to spend some of their free time in CAP's storefront drop-in centers, which are the base of operations for each of the six CAP programs around the state. The storefronts serve as social centers for both CAP youngsters and for their friends. "There's no way to run a storefront for DYS kids unless you've got other kids in there," Wolfe says. "We don't want to segregate DYS kids from everybody else." CAP workers have had to clamp down, however, on some outsiders who were suspected of bringing drugs into the centers. The storefronts—equipped with table tennis, pool tables, and small libraries—are used as offices and meeting rooms for staff members, for recreation and for informal "rap sessions" between youth and staff.

Joey's counselor was Peter Hulett, a twenty-five-year-old former stereo salesman, born and raised in Worcester, a declining industrial city of about 200,000. When Hulett went to work for CAP and Joey was placed in his caseload, his most important immediate goal was to keep Joey away from some of his friends who were incorrigible car thieves. Stealing cars is the principal recreation for most of Worcester's delinquent youth, Hulett says. They will steal anything on wheels. (Massachusetts, according to state officials, has the highest rate of car theft in the nation.)

Hulett's summertime routine was to pick up Joey at the project each morning and either drop him at the Worcester storefront or take the boy with him on his visits to the other four youths in his caseload. Hulett says his relationship with Joey was "a big-brother thing, a trust thing." Joey's parents had difficulty controlling him, Hulett says, and gave Hulett much responsibility for imposing controls. The counselor says, "I don't have much over him except the five-dollar allowance," which all CAP youth receive every week for cooperating with their counselors. He therefore had to rely on a sort of natural rapport with the boy.

When Joey—a chronic truant—returned to school, Hulett dropped him off in the morning and picked him up at night for the first few weeks. After negotiating with the school administration, he got him placed in a special education class. As of September 1976, Joey had kept out of trouble with the authorities for more than a year.

Chapter 5
Closing the Juvenile Institutions

Its opening was proclaimed, by some, a landmark in prison reform. So was its closing—126 years later. The Lyman School for Boys in Westboro, Massachusetts, was the first institution of its kind in the nation. When it was opened, state officials said it placed Massachusetts in the forefront of prison reform. Young lawbreakers were removed from the dank jails and prisons where they had been held up to that time and moved to the wooded countryside where the school was located. There, it was said, they would receive humane but firm care in a healthy rural atmosphere. The year was 1846.

On January 17, 1972, the Lyman School for Boys was closed forever. Its closing was a spectacular event, in which a caravan of cars and motorcycles descended on the institution, picked up the thirty-nine remaining youngsters and sped off to the University of Massachusetts at Amherst, where the youngsters stayed until other homes were found for them.

For years before its closing, reformers had repeatedly denounced Lyman as a brutal and dehumanizing institution, a school of crime whose residents were almost always worse threats to society when they left than when they went in.

The closing of the Lyman School was the finale of an intense drama that had been going on in Massachusetts for more than two years. The era of confining children in large correctional institutions was dead, declared Dr. Jerome Miller, then-commissioner of the Department of Youth Services. He predicted that a new age of decent, humane, community-based care for delinquent youngsters was beginning.

The idealistic young reformers who had worked so hard to close down the institutions cheered. They had initiated a process that came to be known as deinstitutionalization. But juvenile-justice professionals, both in Massachusetts and other states, were stunned and in many cases horrified at what Jerome Miller had done.

Miller and his supporters have been criss-crossing the nation since 1972, trying to persuade other administrators that institutions for juveniles are both destructive and unnecessary, and telling and retelling the story of what Miller has called his great "crusade" in Massachusetts.

Since the time when Jerome Miller shocked the nation by closing Massachusetts' juvenile institutions, the issue of juvenile crime has risen to the top of the agenda of the criminal-justice community. Police officials, politicians and concerned citizens complain that while juveniles commit a disproportionate number of the most violent crimes (murder, rape, armed robbery and assault), judges and corrections officials release most juvenile offenders outright or under probation supervision. And these critics maintain that a lot of the sentences given to juvenile offenders are too lenient.

The press and television have responded by covering the issue heavily, with emphasis on the alleged growth in violent crime by juveniles. But some people may disagree about the interpretation of the statistics. In 1976, for instance, there was much coverage in the New York City media of what state legislators called a tremendous increase in violent crime by juveniles. But an analysis of the figures showed that there had been no increase in murders and assaults by juveniles over the ten-year period from 1965 to 1975. There had been, however, roughly a 260 percent increase in robberies by juveniles.

There is a great ideological abyss between the thinking of the police and their supporters on the one hand and prison reformers like Miller on the other. The police say that any juvenile over the age of fourteen or fifteen who commits a violent crime should be held accountable and punished just like an adult. The reformers say that we cannot judge children in the same way as adults, and that the idea of imprisoning any but the most violent is abhorrent. Instead, they say, everything possible should be done to keep them in their own homes, or in humane, community-based programs, until they reach the age of majority. This is especially true, they argue, for juveniles who are guilty of so-called status offenses —offenses such as truancy, running away from home and "incorrigibility," offenses which do not exist for adults. In some states as many as a third of the children in state institutions are there for status offenses.

The recent clamor to lock up more juvenile offenders conflicts with the prevailing national trend of the last decade. According to a study by the National Assessment of Juvenile Corrections at the University of Michigan, the number of juvenile offenders held in public institutions has markedly declined in the last few years, from 43,000 in 1969 to only 28,000 in 1974. Judges and corrections officials attribute this change to a shift in attitude on their part. They no longer believe, as they once did, that a stint in the state reform school is good for a delinquent youngster, that it will help to change his behavior for the better.

Many now believe that institutions, especially large ones, are profoundly destructive, and they are extremely reluctant to send to an institution any child who is not demonstrably dangerous. Nowhere has this shift in attitudes been more dramatic than in Massachusetts.

The movement to reform the Massachusetts juvenile-justice system actually began in the early sixties. The force behind it then was a number of well-established child-advocacy groups. The reformers charged that the institutions—located at Bridgewater, Shirley, Lyman, Oakdale and Lancaster—were brutal and punitive, that some staff members had regularly beaten and abused many children, that children were locked for long periods of time in segregation cells and improperly fed, that all children had their heads shaved and were forced to march from activity to activity in formation. Treatment, where there was any, was subservient to custody, the reformers maintained.

Little action was taken on these complaints until 1969, when the state legislature passed a bill reorganizing the youth services system. Then-Governor Francis Sargent obtained the resignation of the incumbent commissioner of DYS, who had held the post since 1952, and selected a blue-ribbon panel to make a nationwide search for a replacement. The committee selected Dr. Jerome Miller, an associate professor of social work at Ohio State, who had little experience in corrections and none in state government.

To his supporters Miller was, and still is, a messianic figure, engaged in what he himself once called a "crusade" to close down the nation's juvenile training schools. They laud him as the most charismatic, dynamic, bold and innovative administrator ever to hold a correctional office. To his many opponents, Miller is a vain and arrogant man who pursued his goal of closing the institutions with fanatical zeal. He reduced the Department of Youth Services to a fiscal and administrative shambles, his detractors say, then

103

resigned, leaving the problem of picking up the pieces to his successor.

But even some of Miller's harshest critics admire his single-minded determination to achieve his goal despite tremendous opposition. William Sears, former superintendent of Massachusetts' maximum-security training school at Bridgewater, is no admirer of Miller, but describes him as "one of the gutsiest people I have ever met in my life." In person, Jerome Miller does not fit the image of a fire-and-brimstone crusader for reform. He is blond, in his mid-forties and still boyish-looking. Slightly overweight and with a disarmingly friendly smile, he is soft-spoken and academic in conversation. He is extremely well read in corrections, and constantly cites the most recent studies to support his arguments.

Miller, born and raised in rural Minnesota, entered the missionary order of the Maryknoll Fathers upon graduation from high school. He left the order after five years with a bachelor's degree in philosophy, having decided not to enter the priesthood.

After receiving a master's degree in social work, Miller enlisted in the Air Force, where he spent ten years, several of them running social-service and mental-health programs in England for Air Force personnel stationed in Europe. Then he became chief of research for the Maryland Department of Juvenile Services, where his peripatetic career in corrections began. After only six weeks he resigned his job, when "it became very, very clear to me that that system was not [concerned with] any basic change."

Miller went to Ohio State, where as a consultant to the Ohio Youth Commission he got his first close look at American training schools. He was horrified, and he brought that horror with him when he went to Massachusetts.

The Massachusetts' juvenile institutions, he says, "were awful. I mean, they were really brutal and terrible places, and I got very involved in looking at that. I'd show up unannounced and look at it [and know] that it was mine and I had to do something about it. I can understand why administrators hide out in their offices, because [looking at the system] shakes your damn ego. It shakes your whole being, and to the degree that you touch it, you have to claim it, and to the degree that you claim it, you're just overwhelmed because you have none of the handles to change it."

Miller says that he had no plans to dismantle the system when he took office. Instead, his intention was to reform the system. The reforms he proposed, most of them involving the revision of institutional rules to give youths more responsibility for their own behavior, were neither new nor particularly radical. Several other states—including Florida, Minnesota, California and New York—were successfully instituting similar plans at that time.

But in Massachusetts the series of edicts issued from Miller's office caused a great stir. The operation of the institutions had remained unchanged for many years, and the individual institutions had operated almost independently from the central administration. As the number of directives increased, so did the anger and resentment of some institutional staff. Miller got an inkling of what was to come when he issued one of his first directives saying that youngsters in the institutions had the right to wear their hair as they chose. The order caused a storm of protest among institution staff members.

During his first year in office Miller also issued directives prohibiting institution staff from striking youths (corporal punishment was not against the law in Massachusetts), permitting youths to wear their own rather than institutional clothing, and prohibiting staff from forcing youths to walk in silent formation from one activity to another. He also forbade the practice of making youngsters in the various disciplinary units sit in silence for hours at a time, and tightened the screening procedures for sending youths to such units.

Miller says that his first year in office was a frustrating time, partly because the legislature had reorganized youth services without providing enough central office funds. Miller's own position was not funded when he took office. He says, "I had to freeze other [job] slots to pay my own salary." There was no money to fill vacant positions with persons of his own choosing, he says. Most of the career civil servants who were on institution staffs had, according to Miller and others, gotten their jobs through political patronage. The average age of staff members at Shirley was fifty-five, Miller says, and was only slightly lower at the other institutions.

Toward the end of his first year in office, new state and federal funds became available. Miller began using these funds to fill vacant positions in the central office, and the institutions with people who shared his philosophy. Most of them had little or no experience in corrections.They came from the state departments of Mental Health and of Public Welfare, from private child care and advocacy groups, and from the vast Massachusetts university community.

Many of these people, especially those from the universities, would normally not have been attracted to jobs in state government, and in fact never intended to pursue careers in corrections. They were young and idealistic and saw their principal job as helping Miller to battle against the entrenched bureaucracy that he charged was trying to sabotage his reforms.

Miller says that he is "very leery of anyone who's had experience in corrections because it very often means one year's experience twenty times over instead of twenty years' experience." He says that those who work in institutions become "self-socialized" so that they do not see the destructive effects the institutions are having on the kids.

The sudden, drastic liberalization of institution rules, and the prohibition of traditional modes of control, caused considerable disruption in the Massachusetts institutions. There were mass runaways, fires and vandalism.

Miller and his adherents maintained that most of the disruption was "staff-stimulated." Some older staff, in an effort to embarrass him, encouraged the youngsters to run away, Miller charged. When incidents occurred, it was alleged that the first thing the staff did was call the newspapers and television stations.

Former institution staff members contended that while there was a limited amount of deliberate sabotage by some staff, most of the disruptions were natural outgrowths of the Miller reforms. These staff members said that some youngsters believed, with some justification, that they could run away and openly defy staff members with impunity, since Miller had forbidden the use of traditional punishments except in extreme cases. They also knew, the former staff argued, that if a youth and staff member gave differing accounts of an incident, Miller's inclination was to accept the youth's version.

Deinstitutionalization

Jerome Miller is not a patient man. He says that after a year in office, he felt he had accomplished very little because of fiscal restraints and institutional staff resistance to his reforms. He was convinced that "kids were still being bounced off the wall" in the various institutions.

The institution that concerned Miller the most was the Institute for Juvenile Guidance at Bridgewater, a 110-year-old, walled former women's prison. It held those youngsters deemed dangerous or unmanageable by the other, more open, institutions. Bridgewater has been the focus of several pre-Miller investigations because of alleged brutality by

107

some staff. Miller made frequent unannounced visits there. During one visit in August 1970, Miller and Mrs. Jessie Sargent, who accompanied him, witnessed an escape attempt by three youths. When the youths were caught, Miller and Mrs. Sargent say, they were beaten by staff members. Two weeks later Miller closed the institution, citing the alleged brutality and saying that in any case, there was no need for such an institution. Most of the sixty boys in the institution were sent home. Twelve—who, it was agreed, presented a threat to themselves or to others—were placed in a secure cottage at the Lyman School.

By early 1971 Miller had decided that all of the institutions must be eliminated. This decision was inspired, first, by his frustration with the pace of reform, and second, by his fear that because of the controversy he had caused, his days in Massachusetts were numbered. "We decided that because of all that backlash, because of all that upset, that probably I and my staff weren't going to survive. . . . It was very clear that we were a liability to the governor. . . . I once hinted at resigning and I didn't get a 'Please don't.' "

In March, Miller paroled all the boys, who ranged in age from seven to twelve, at the institution at Oakdale, and converted it to a reception center. At the same time he instituted plans to phase out the Industrial School at Shirley.

During 1971 Miller stepped up what was already a vigorous "public information" campaign. Throughout his administration he was constantly speaking to civic, church and university groups. He made frequent appearances on radio and television, held several meetings with the editorial board of the Boston *Globe*, which strongly supported him, and invited reporters to tour his facilities.

Miller usually took several youngsters, sometimes dozens, to his public appearances. Miller would condemn his own institutions, and then invite the young wards of those institutions to do likewise. Most of the meetings focused on brutality and violence. The youngsters told of having their heads beaten against stone walls by staff members, of having their faces shoved into toilet bowls or into their own feces, or of being locked naked for days in segregation cells.

Miller's public-information campaign did not endear him to the institution staff, though he insists today that it was not directed at particular staff members, or even at his own institutions. "I think most places that house juveniles are underneath [it all] brutal," he says. "I think that large institutions with coerced populations are based in violence. That doesn't mean that everybody is going around beating kids. . . .

"I always make clear, but people never hear me, [that there is a] difference between a system that brings out the worst impulses in people, and people who are bad."

In December 1971 Miller closed the Industrial School for Boys at Shirley, sending most of the fifty remaining children home and transferring the rest to Lyman. At the start of 1972, the only remaining training schools were Lyman and Lancaster. Plans for the closing of Lyman began only twenty days before the event. Students from the University of Massachusetts at Amherst, the school which was most active on Miller's behalf, executed the operation. The principal organizer was Larry Dye, a graduate student, ex-convict and founder of the Juvenile Opportunities Extension (JOE), a voluntary student organization that provided tutoring and other services to delinquents from the western part of Massachusetts. Edward Budelman, then a doctoral candidate in education and later an assistant commissioner of the Department of Youth Services, assisted Dye.

Miller asked Budelman and his Amherst friends to help with the closing of the Lyman School, a task which Budelman took on with relish, especially after he spent a few days living in the institution. "When I walked into the disciplinary cottage at Lyman the first time," he says, "there were

109

sixteen kids sitting there in their underpants with their arms folded across their chests, sitting in steel chairs, at attention. They weren't saying a word and the supervisor was sitting in the back of the room with a loaded .38 right out there on the desk. That's what we were running."

Budelman suggested to Miller that "the only chance to close the last big place was to do it in a day. So I said why don't we descend on it with two hundred college students" and take all the remaining youngsters to Amherst. This became the plan.

When the caravan of cars arrived on January 17 and took the youngsters away, the reaction of Lyman's staff was utter disbelief. "Staff there had been told months before that the institution would be closed," according to one study of Miller's administration, "but simply could not believe it. A cottage that had [previously] burned was painstakingly rebuilt by staff, who were standing at the door waiting for youth to be assigned the day the motorcade to Amherst virtually emptied the institution in a matter of hours."

The thirty-nine youngsters from Lyman were joined at Amherst by sixty others from Lancaster and the "reception" units of the detention and reception centers at Westfield and Roslindale. At this point the only sentenced youngsters remaining in Massachusetts institutions for juveniles were about twenty girls, who occupied one cottage at Lancaster. Because DYS had great difficulty finding community programs for delinquent girls, this cottage remained open until July 1974, when it too was closed, and the last vestige of the old training-school system disappeared.

The Aftermath

It has often been charged that Miller gave little thought to exactly what kind of system would replace the state institutions. Miller points out, however, that he had a team of planners working on the development of a network of community programs as early as January 1971. When he decided to close the institutions later in that year, the planning group, which eventually grew to twenty-four members, quickly came up with a master plan for the community placement of the youngsters.

The planners' two main recommendations were 1) that the great bulk of services be purchased by contract from private agencies, and 2) that the delivery of services be almost totally regionalized, with the regional staff making all the decisions about the placement of individual children.

Miller had already set up seven regional offices, staffed with former institution employees, prior to the closing of the Lyman and Shirley institutions.

The planning group's recommendation for purchase of service fit perfectly with Miller's conviction that state bureaucracies were inherently incapable of providing quality services to delinquents—or to any other people placed in their care. Furthermore, Miller's top deputy, Joseph Leavey, had worked for years in the state Department of Public Welfare, which has a long history of purchasing care for its juvenile wards.

Miller elevates the issue of private versus public care to the sociopolitical realm. Public institutions have always been reserved for the poor, he says, and the poor have had no other option. "If there is a model for care," he adds, "it's the model that's always existed for the upper middle class. There have been for the last one hundred years decent ways of treating dangerous rich kids."

What Miller originally had in mind to replace the institutions was a network of small, privately operated group homes. During fiscal 1972, he obtained federal funds to operate thirteen such facilities, and state money to establish several more. When the institutions closed, there was enough bed space for between two and three hundred youths in the group homes; DYS needed space for at least double that many.

Throughout his campaign to close the institutions, Miller contended that taxpayers' money—as much as $10,000 a year per child—was being wasted on custodial care in institutions, when good community care could be provided at a much lower cost. Miller's figures are still hotly contested, with his critics arguing that the $10,000 figure was based on the cost of running institutions which, under Miller, were only at a third of their capacity. They say that the cost of running the institutions in 1967, when they were full, was $3,000–$4,000 per child.

Also, though Miller's initial agreements with the group homes provided for them to be paid $3,000–$5,000 a year per child, it soon became apparent that this figure was much too low. Group homes now operated by DYS cost a minimum of $10,000 a year per child. Miller says today that he has stopped telling people that community programs are less expensive than institutions. "I wouldn't make that argument any more—that it should be done on the grounds that it's cheaper. I would say that whatever resources we are putting into large institutions would be better spent putting the same money into community-based programs. You get more bang for the buck, if you will."

The group homes presented other administrative problems. Attempts to establish them in stable residential communities often met with insurmountable community resistance. As a result, most were established in low-income and industrial neighborhoods or, ironically, in empty buildings on the grounds of state institutions, including Lancaster.

The most serious problem with the group homes was that many youths would not stay in them, officials of the Miller period say. They ran away in droves and were often passed from one group home to another, running away from each in turn.

The culture in the institutions where most of the youths had come from, says William Madaus, one of Miller's aides at the time, fostered a minimum of intimacy among the youths and between youths and staff. This carried over, he says, "and the youths hated the community facilities. They would flee most quickly from the best programs, where there was a lot of intimacy." As a result, Madaus adds, there was "tremendous chaos" in the community programs for more than two years—until the former residents of the institutions were too old to remain in DYS custody.

Madaus says that if he had it to do over, "I would not have touched the kids in the institutions. I would have let the kids finish their time and paroled them, and set up a reception facility to introduce new kids to the community setting."

Miller has since concluded that the emphasis on group homes was his biggest mistake. "We didn't believe our own rhetoric [about the value of nonresidential facilities]," he says. "We really believed that the kids in institutions needed residential care, and I guess for political reasons we wanted to establish that."

Because of the problems in establishing and running the group homes, and because there were not nearly enough of them to absorb all DYS commitments, Miller and his successors ended up relying much more than anticipated on nonresidential programs.

Throughout his administration, Miller's greatest struggle was to find money to implement his reforms. He had virtually no state funds for planning, regionalization, program development, program monitoring and evaluation, and very little money for purchase of care. When he closed the institutions, he at first anticipated being able to transfer the money used to operate them to pay for community programs, but this never worked out. When he left office in January 1973, DYS was still paying $2.7 million a year to

113

maintain the institutions, even though they were closed. And most of the institution staff members were still on the DYS payroll, many of them working in the seven newly established regional offices.

Despite the shortage of money there was a constant, almost frantic search for new programs. It is said that almost anyone, whatever his credentials, could walk into Miller's office, propose a program, get it verbally approved on the spot and start receiving youths the same day. The only condition was that the program would have to wait for funding, sometimes many months.

Joseph Leavey, the man who was in charge of developing new programs, says that more than two hundred were launched in a single year, including group homes, boarding schools, nonresidential programs and foster homes, and "shelter care" facilities for those awaiting trial. Established child-care agencies ran some of the programs, but most were run by fledgling community agencies, student groups and ex-offender organizations. Leavey says today that many of these programs turned out to be fiscally unstable and of questionable quality, and went out of business fairly quickly. The problem was that "they were really basing the whole thing on enthusiasm," Leavey says, "and the problem with enthusiasm is that it runs out." But these programs, he adds, made an important contribution during the period of transition from a totally institutional system to a totally community-based one.

Much of the money for the establishment of the community system came from a single source: the Governor's Committee on Public Safety, the state agency that disburses federal Law Enforcement Assistance Administration (LEAA) funds. During fiscal years 1971 and 1972, DYS received grants of almost $1.5 million from the committee. Every year since then it has received over $1 million to help implement and operate its community programs.

114

From Miller's standpoint, the most important function served by the federal money was to permit him to fund the operation of regional offices and private programs without having to lay off or fire existing staff. In fact, during his entire administration Miller did not lay off or fire a single DYS employee. Without federal money he would have had to free the available state funds by furloughing or firing hundreds of employees, which, he says, "would have led to a great massacre, mainly of me."

By far the most serious charges against Miller, from both his enemies and supporters, concern his implementation and management of the community programs. One government report labeled his administration "enlightened philosophy—fiscal and administrative chaos."

Former Assistant Commissioner Budelman comments, "I love him. He's a brilliant guy . . . , a charismatic guy that really cares about kids. But if you want structure and organization, he's not your man. The administrative ability may or may not be there."

There are those who charge that Miller's temper, his penchant for showmanship, and his determination to achieve one goal—the closing of the institutions—got in the way of good administration. Miller had a "tendency to create the polarized position," says Albert Kramer, who was Governor Sargent's chief policy adviser, so that he didn't have to negotiate with opponents of his programs. Kramer, who became a state district court judge, adds that "It's so nice to be the good guy versus the villain. He is always better in war than in peace. I think he has his limitations in peace. . . .

"What we had was a very strong guy who created the magic but couldn't put a system around the magic, which is not a very romantic thing to do anyway. The dreamers, who love to deal with magic all the time, they love him. The

115

people who see it as black magic, they hate him."

Kramer was Miller's chief liaison with the governor and worked closely with him to try to work out some of his administrative and fiscal problems. Though still a Miller admirer, Kramer's assessment is that "the man, because of inadequacies either in himself or in the people he hired, failed to get control of his system [after the training schools were closed] and move it along. . . . That's the hard work." In short, Kramer says, "I don't think he's a long-distance runner." If he had it to do over again, Kramer says, "I'd pitch him for five innings and go to my bullpen. I think he went eight."

Miller denies that he was incapable of administering the new system after he succeeded in getting the institutions closed. The reason he didn't stay around to consolidate and build community programs, he says, is because the "roles are quite different. It's very difficult to establish new programs and get them going, and at the same time, have to continue in the role of the sustainer of the [same] programs, because the people that have to sustain it are the people whose toes you've stepped on to establish it."

Miller adds that the kind of battle he fought in Massachusetts takes a large personal toll. "I'm not sure I would want to run a long way under those pressures. The personal pressures make it impossible. I think if you don't stir up those pressures, you can run a very long distance. The average bureaucrat is a very long distance runner."

Miller continued to be controversial after he left Massachusetts in January 1973. He says he was "seduced" to Illinois by Governor Dan Walker, who appointed him director of the Department of Family and Children's Services, which handles abused, neglected and abandoned children. Miller says he took the job on the condition that responsibility for delinquent youth, who are under the Department of

Corrections, would be transferred to his department. They weren't, and Walker finally fired Miller in August 1974.

After his "very unpleasant" experience in Illinois, Miller went to Pennsylvania, where in mid-1976, he was still commissioner of the Office of Children and Youth, which handles Pennsylvania's delinquent youngsters. Again Miller focused on the heart of the system. He closed off admissions to the maximum-security facility for juveniles at Camp Hill. And again Miller is under attack for allegedly poor management, for moving too fast and for failing to consult other officials, especially the judges, before acting.

Miller says that he would like to make Pennsylvania his "last state," that the controversy that surrounds him wherever he goes takes too much out of him physically and emotionally. But he is widely regarded as the chief spokesman—perhaps the only well-known national spokesman—for the movement to tear down the walls of juvenile correctional institutions. He claims that this role of crusader for reform has been thrust upon him almost against his will—that he is "uncomfortable" in it.

"In a sense I got caught up in [that role] and I'm stuck with it now," he says. "And I feel a certain responsibility to it now, so that I can't really walk away from it. Any time you walk away from it you're considered a failure, and more important, what you've done is considered a failure. So, in a sense, you're kind of a victim of your own success."

Jerome Miller is a renegade among juvenile corrections administrators. While most other administrators favor the maximum use of community programs for delinquent youngsters, no others appear to favor doing away with institutions altogether, as Miller is.

Many other administrators also disagree with Miller's argument that all institutions are by their very nature destructive and violent. They say that there are some extremely

117

successful experiments going on with the very concept that Miller tried unsuccessfully to implement in the Massachusetts institutions—the therapeutic community. Dozens of juvenile institutions all over the country have been converted into therapeutic communities.

The treatment offered in these institutions goes by various names—Guided Group Interaction (GGI), Positive Peer Culture, Reality Therapy—but is often referred to by practitioners as simply "the group method." Though the group method was born more than twenty years ago at the well-known Highfields project for juveniles in New Jersey, it has only become a national phenomenon in the last ten years.

In every place where it is used, the major thrust is to turn over responsibility for behavior, for the reinforcement of positive attitudes, and for performance in educational and other programs to the youngsters themselves. Sanctions are applied and individual problems discussed at frequent group meetings. Powers and duties traditionally reserved for professional staff are turned over to the delinquents; the role of adults is simply to "guide" the process.

Many of those who have adopted the group method report what they consider to be astonishing changes in the behavior and attitudes of delinquents. The method is in use in at least ten states: New Jersey, Minnesota, South Dakota, West Virginia, Illinois, Georgia, New Hampshire, Florida, Maryland and Michigan. In several states it is the only mode of treatment in juvenile institutions.

Though there has been no recent study of the group method that is acceptable to social scientists, many administrators are convinced beyond a doubt of its effectiveness. Says Gerald Hicks, director of Michigan's Office of Children and Youth Services, "I'm inclined to think that a group process is the best for a high percentage of kids. . . . There has been a real searching by people in juvenile delinquency programs for something that will work. And this is as close as we've ever gotten to something that works. It draws on the real power base in the institution—the strength of the kid-to-kid relationship."

Says Gordon Faulkner, head of West Virginia's Division of Correction, "I have a great deal of confidence that we can affect the recidivism rate [with the group method]. I really do not doubt that if we can properly implement it, we can effect change with the majority of young people that come into the system."

Other administrators are not willing to go so far. In Illinois, two institutions had adopted the method by mid-1976. Director Samuel Sublett of the Juvenile Division says, "GGI is no panacea and it's not appropriate for all kids. It's an effective tool for dealing with your staff and it's an institutional control."

In the Highfields facility, at exactly 7 P.M., Eddie, dressed in jeans and T-shirt, walked into the office and sat down heavily in a metal folding chair. It was Eddie's "meeting" tonight, and he wasn't in the mood. Moments later, eight other boys filed in and took their positions in a circle.

"Anybody got any raps on 'im?" someone asked, and suddenly Eddie was on the firing line. Eddie left "crusty stuff" all over a pot he was washing, said one boy. He didn't clean up the table when he was serving, said another. He "agitated" another boy while he was on the phone. He didn't try to break up a fight between a black and a white boy. He didn't try often enough to "help guys with their problems." Eddie denied everything and cursed his accusors. There was a great deal of shouting.

Eddie, an admitted drug addict, purse snatcher, burglar and armed robber, was merely having his monthly group meeting at Highfields, New Jersey's well-known project for delinquents, where Eddie had been for four months. He was one of eighteen boys in residence, all aged sixteen and seventeen. All of them had been given suspended reformatory sentences by judges who thought they might benefit from what has become known across the nation as the "Highfields concept."

Highfields provides a program of "guided group interaction" in which the delinquents are responsible for their own reform. They make and enforce many of the rules governing the house they live in. Located deep in the woods in Hopewell, New Jersey, the house was donated to the state by Charles Lindbergh. (It is the house from which Lindbergh's infant son was kidnapped in 1932.) The boys sleep on bunks in two-man rooms in a section of the house that used to be the garage. There are no bars and no locked doors. They can run away at will, but it's a long walk home, and when they are caught, chances are good they will be sent to a reformatory.

All of the boys must work at menial labor in a nearby mental hospital. The labor is intended to teach good work habits; they are paid nominal wages.

Every night there are two "meetings," each lasting about an hour and a half and each focusing on a particular boy. The first part of the meeting is the most raucous. The subject's peers are required to "rat" on him if he has broken any of the house rules since his last meeting. To hold back any accusation is called "cliquing" and is considered a serious infraction in itself. When the ratting is done, the delinquent/therapists begin discussing, much more calmly, what in previous meetings they have formally identified as the boy's "problems."

The meetings are considered the best way for the boys and their adult supervisors to learn whether a delinquent's attitudes toward himself, his peers, his parents and his criminal activity have significantly changed. One of the best methods of measuring such changes is to examine a boy's behavior during a weekend furlough at home. Most of the boys, who stay about four months before being paroled, get at least two such furloughs while at Highfields.

Superintendent Albert Axelrod, who has run Highfields for eighteen years, says that 50 to 60 percent of those who complete the program do not make a new appearance in juvenile court during the twelve months following their release; 40 to 50 percent get into new trouble with the law within a year; and only 10 to 15 percent commit new offenses for which they are sent to prison.

New Jersey officials have duplicated the program in three other rural locations around the state.

Back in 1967, after officials of the Minnesota Department of Corrections concluded that the inmates in their correctional institutions were "sick," they instituted the "medical model" of treatment. One institution where they set out to make inmates "well" was the State Training School at Red Wing. The co-ed institution for juveniles was virtually taken over by a team of three psychiatrists and five psychologists, says Red Wing's superintendent, Milton Olson. The result was "a hell of a lot of trouble." Olson says the doctors and psychologists were "dishing out pills like they were going out of style." They gave the juvenile inmates almost complete freedom, which "demoralized" the staff. And, he adds, there was "no real impact except that it gave the kids a license to run amok."

In August 1968, Olson says, "it blew up." During that month a hundred youngsters ran away from the institution. There was also a small riot, in which the youths occupied Red Wing's security cottage.

The Department of Corrections quickly abandoned the medical model. In September 1968 it hired a consultant to help reorganize the institution. He introduced the treatment method still in use—Positive Peer Culture (PPC). Red

Wing was the first correctional institution in the country to adopt PPC as its main treatment method.

The purpose of the PPC program—and all Guided Group Interaction programs—is to undermine the destructive, criminal subculture which prevails at most correctional institutions. Before the introduction of PPC, Olson says, relationships among Red Wing residents were controlled by the "bully system," in which the physically strongest delinquents held sway over the weaker, younger boys. PPC, he says, forced residents to relate to each other more positively.

The problems with which each Red Wing inmate is expected to deal are formally identified when he enters the institution and tells his "life story" to his or her treatment group. PPC recognizes nine kinds of problems, the most common of which are resentment of authority, feelings of inferiority, drinking, drugs and family trouble.

Red Wing residents who were interviewed all said they liked the Positive Peer Culture program. One youth who had been in and out of institutions for four years said that the program had taught him to "go positive" in his relationships with his family, teachers and other authority figures. Another said he thought that when released, he would be less likely to turn to drugs every time something went wrong. All said they felt much more comfortable discussing their problems with their peers than they had ever felt discussing them with adults.

The staff is also very enthusiastic about the program, though Superintendent Olson admits that it is no longer as popular as it once was among top Minnesota officials. Olson claims that eight out of every ten juveniles released from the program stay out of trouble for twelve months after their release, and that the success rate over two to three years is better than 60 percent. Other officials question these statistics, and suggest that there should be an alternative to the

PPC program for juveniles sent to Red Wing. John Maloney, education director at the adult prison at Stillwater, who taught school for five years at Red Wing, says that the PPC mandatory participation rule is "like trying to fit everybody into a size eight shoe."

Chapter 6
Is Rehabilitation Dead?

In 1870 a group of prison administrators from all over the world met in Cincinnati, Ohio. The occasion was the first Congress of the National Prison Association, forerunner of the American Correctional Association. Participants in the congress later described it as a "mountain-top" experience, in which wardens, guards and ardent prison reformers, including such celebrities as Florence Nightingale, joined forces to endorse a new Declaration of Principles for the operation of the prison system.

The purpose of imprisonment should no longer be "vindictive punishment," the declaration announced, but the "reformation" of criminals. "Granite walls and iron bars, although they deprive the criminal of his liberty and inflict a just physical punishment," declared the keynote speaker, "do not work that reformation in the soul of the man that will restore him to society regenerated and reformed."

Participants in the Congress were sent back to their prisons with the following invocation from the Reverend E. C. Wines, one of the event's organizers: "Let us, then, go down from these heights of social, intellectual and spiritual enjoyment, to toil faithfully, resolutely, persistently in our respective fields of labor, and so fulfill the high mission assigned to us by Providence—the regeneration and redemption of fallen humanity."

And that is exactly what prison administrators and reformers have been trying to do ever since—though perhaps with less of the religious fervor that characterized the 1870 congress. The question, of course, is how exactly to go about achieving the "regeneration and redemption" of the criminal offender.

Before the 1870 congress, the purpose of imprisonment was punishment. Backbreaking labor, the lock step, the rule of silence, constant religious instruction, and for those who transgressed while in prison, brutal beatings and solitary confinement were the rule. After 1870 the model was the "reformatory," in which inmates were subject to less brutal discipline, and through hard work and good behavior, could work their way out of prison through parole.

During the post–World War II era, more modern theories of rehabilitation took hold. The road to redemption was through education and vocational training or through psychological counseling, or through a combination of those elements. Finally, in the last ten years, the contemporary counterparts of the 1870 reformers concluded that it was the prison itself that was the chief obstacle to rehabilitation. What was needed, the reformers declared, was to keep the great majority of criminal offenders in their own communities, where they could work, support their families and be spared the socially debilitating effect of imprisonment altogether.

Until recent years there was very little hard evidence concerning the effectiveness of any of the various approaches to rehabilitation. Corrections administrators could

125

boast of the efficacy of educational programs, counseling or community-based treatment, or even work in the cotton fields, without fear of contradiction.

But since the mid-fifties the body of research on correctional programing has grown. And in 1974 a professor of sociology at New York's City College, Dr. Robert Martinson, issued a summary that analyzed the results of a wide array of correctional projects conducted from the mid-forties through 1967. His conclusion rocked the academic and professional corrections communities. He said, in effect, that nothing works—that "with few and isolated exceptions, the rehabilitation efforts that have been reported so far have had no appreciable effect on recidivism"—the propensity of released offenders to commit new crimes.

The Martinson study, and the results of similar research by other academics and some corrections administrators, set off an intense debate. Most administrators vigorously defended the value of their programs. They questioned the accuracy and the methods of the research and publicly expressed fears that politicians would pick up the Martinson findings and try to use them to destroy programs the administrators had struggled for years to establish.

Inevitably the debate made its way into the political arena. Politicians, citing rising crime rates along with the negative results of rehabilitation research, demanded that more criminals be locked up and locked up longer. One of the first politicians to adopt this position was then-U.S. Attorney General William Saxbe.

In late 1974 Saxbe began barnstorming the nation with speeches attacking lenient judges and a prosecutorial system that, he said, resulted in many offenders going free undeservedly or serving sentences that were too short. Saxbe also denounced the entire prison reform movement. He said it had led to the diversion and early release from prisons of tens of thousands of dangerous criminals.

He declared that he had once been a supporter of rehabilitation programs and of the diversion of offenders to community programs and probation. But in his most widely publicized speech, in September 1974, Saxbe said he had been wrong. He pronounced rehabilitation a "myth," at least for violent criminals, his definition of anyone from a murderer to a burglar. The solution to the crime problem was not more rehabilitation programs, he maintained, but more punishment. "I think that punishment has a place," he said in one speech, "and if you catch people and you prosecute them and you punish them, it is a deterrent to crime."

Saxbe's contention that rehabilitation programs don't work might not have made such an impact if it had not been accompanied by similar statements from dozens of others in the criminal-justice community. All at once, it seemed, everyone, from the International Association of Chiefs of Police to the American Friends Service Committee, was declaring rehabilitation a failure.

The Martinson Study

Robert Martinson came to his startling conclusion after studying data on the results of 231 programs operated around the country from 1945 to 1967. While Martinson was quick to point out that the data he looked at covered only a tiny minority of the programs under way then or initiated since, he believed that his findings obligated administrators to prove that rehabilitation programs currently in operation were effective, to justify them on other grounds or to eliminate them.

How strong is the evidence that correctional programs do not work? And what do researchers like Martinson mean when they make that assertion? Do they mean that educational programs do not educate, that therapy and counseling programs do not change attitudes, that drug programs do

127

not curb addiction, that employment programs do not lead anywhere, that behavior-modification programs do not change people?

The answer is no. When researchers and other experts say the programs are failures, what they almost always mean is that they are ineffective at reducing recidivism. And by recidivism they mean the rate at which offenders return to criminal activity, not institutions, after they have been released from a correctional program.

Few deny that many correctional programs are effective in achieving their immediate goals. There is considerable evidence, says Martinson, that well-run remedial education programs do succeed at teaching many illiterate offenders to read and write, that vocational training programs do produce thousands of competent welders, auto mechanics, plumbers, electricians and computer programmers. Tests administered to offenders who have gone through counseling and therapy programs indicate that some do emerge with more constructive, less hostile attitudes.

When such programs were widely introduced, in the fifties in some states and in the sixties in others, it was assumed by most administrators that the programs could not help but reduce recidivism. But research studies as early as 1957 disclosed that there was no significant difference on parole between those who had gone through the programs and those who had not. It was assumed by administrators that this was because there were flaws in the programs, and they redoubled their efforts to get more funding and better staff.

When the research studies, many of them done in California, continued to indicate that the programs were not working, many criminologists and administrators decided that the problem was the harsh and sterile conditions in the institutions themselves. In order for the programs to work, reformers argued, they must be conducted either in small humane institutions or in the community.

Millions and millions of dollars were appropriated to build smaller institutions and to start community programs. The federal Law Enforcement Assistance Administration (LEAA) has funneled $1.5 billion of federal money into this effort. The ultimate goal was to reduce crime, or at least to reduce the likelihood that offenders who went through the new programs would commit new crimes after they were released. There were many who said that humanitarian grounds alone justified the reforms and changes, but when it came to convincing Congress and the state legislatures to appropriate new money, the most powerful argument was that the new institutions and programs would reduce recidivism. Since most crime is committed by repeaters, the experts argued, to reduce recidivism was to reduce crime.

But the programs have done neither, say Martinson, Saxbe and a host of other criminal-justice professionals. These and other critics now contend that the primary purpose of corrections should again be what it was for most of the nation's history—punishment, deterrence and incapacitation.

Those who dispute Martinson's findings argue that he overdrew his conclusions and that all the anguish over the effectiveness of programs is unnecessary. Their argument runs this way: Martinson's study examines research on programs conducted before 1967. It was only after 1967 that the prison reform movement got into full swing. Until that time, programs—where there were any—were disorganized and understaffed, or staffed by people who were poorly paid and for the most part even more poorly trained. Community programs, compared to today, were almost nonexistent in most states. LEAA, which funded, and still funds, many community programs, did not even exist until 1968. Furthermore, one of the areas in which corrections was most deficient prior to 1967 was research. (Martinson is the first to admit this. In examining the literature on corrections programs between 1945 and 1967, he came up with more than 1,200 studies, of which only 231 included data that were "interpretable.") Martinson's critics also said that he ended up examining data on so few programs in different categories that to extend his conclusions to all such programs made no sense.

Martinson acknowledges that his study was limited and that the press may have oversimplified and magnified his conclusions. For instance, he states that he has never said that there is no treatment program in operation anywhere that is effective. "I couldn't possibly say that because I haven't looked at all treatment programs everywhere," or even at a representative sample of programs. His study "is not a sample of programs," he adds. "It is a sample of research studies on programs. . . . Our studies ended in December 1967. How do I know that the next two hundred studies won't show tremendous success?"

Martinson also cautions that there were several kinds of programs not included in his research, either because they didn't exist or because they had never been studied before 1967. They include work-release, pre-trial diversion, methadone maintenance and many other kinds of programs that have proliferated in recent years.

Another correctional researcher, Dr. Ted Palmer of the California Youth Authority, wrote a critique of Martinson's study, in which he points out that Martinson, in describing his findings, often states that the results were "equivocal" and the evidence "sparse." Martinson also cites evidence that some programs do work for some offenders, Palmer adds. Palmer contends that Martinson was looking for a single program that would work for everyone, and that because he didn't find it, declared the field bankrupt.

"People Can Be Helped . . ."

Prison administrators agree with Palmer that many of their critics are looking for a single program that will be effective for everyone. In late 1975 *Corrections Magazine* conducted a survey of all eighty-four top prison administrators in the nation. Asked if they thought corrections programs were effective, more than 60 percent answered yes, but many qualified their statements with a single phrase: "There is no panacea."

"People can be helped, can be remotivated," said Amos Reed, then head of the Oregon prison system and now deputy director of adult corrections in Florida. "They can be taught to read if they couldn't read. A harelip can be mended. All kinds of things can be modified and ameliorated. Self-image can be improved. This does not mean that they cease to have the passions, the primitive urges, the capacity to strike out and make errors in judgment. Those still continue. But it's wrong to get into the bag of all or nothing at all."

Said Corrections Director George Denton of Ohio: "From my experience over twenty-five years, I feel that certain programs in institutions *have* helped offenders' reintegration into the community. . . . Vocational training, basic education, completion of high school diploma, college training courses, post-educational and work-release [are all effective programs]. I have employed thirty-two ex-offenders in the department's ex-offender program, and I hear these individuals state that there was something positive in the [institutional] programs."

Perhaps the most enthusiastic argument that programs have worked has come from Nolan Ellandson, former director of corrections in Iowa. "Something works for everybody," he said. "That's our job—to find out what works for each person. . . . It might be the guards, it might be the walls and the bars, it might be the math teacher, or it might be some program."

Joseph Vitek, director of the Department of Correctional Services in Nebraska, said: "[Programs] do work. What some people are saying is that nothing works. But any thorough investigation would show that it does work to a high degree, especially if the control group is a 100 per cent failure. There are dramatic examples of rehabilitation. The people who are saying nothing works are really not people who are knowledgeable."

While the majority of adult administrators defended their prison programs, they said at the same time that they didn't need to prove that programs have worked to justify the existence of prisons.

"For the past several years, particularly since Attica," said Norman Carlson, director of the U.S. Bureau of Prisons, "prisons have been viewed as places of rehabilitation. Somehow the notion is conveyed that that's what their primary objective ought to be—really their only objective in the eyes of some."

Carlson believes that prisons have three objectives: "deterrence, retribution, and rehabilitation. Rehabilitation took on an aura that it's the most important of those three, when in reality it's not. I always tell judges you should never send a man to prison so he can be rehabilitated. If rehabilitation is your goal, it ought to be done in the community."

Juvenile administrators were even more emphatic than their colleagues in adult corrections in declaring that programs could change delinquent behavior. And, in fact, the researchers and reformers who have declared that programs don't work have been referring generally to adult offenders. Even Martinson said that there is some evidence that juveniles have been more amenable to treatment than adults, and that some programs have shown positive results.

Samuel Sublett, Jr., director of the Juvenile Division of the Illinois Department of Corrections, summed up the feeling of most juvenile administrators: "When we're talking about people in the early stages of development, we can't say there is no possibility of rehabilitation. I don't think growth ever really stops until you go to that valley of the shadows."

The administrator who seemed most upset by the controversy over the validity of correctional programs was Allen Breed, director of the California Youth Authority. He has administered one of the nation's largest juvenile systems, with four thousand offenders. "Rehabilitation as a specific strategy for delinquent kids *has* failed in that we are not able to put [all] kids in a specific program and change their behavior patterns," Breed said. "But you can't then make the step and say that nothing in corrections works! Specific programs aimed at specific kids *have* shown positive results. . . . I'm convinced that we have early indications that we can help kids." He cited as examples two Youth Authority institutions in Stockton, California, one of which adopted a behavior-modification, token-economy program, and the other, transactional analysis. A study by the Youth Authority and the National Institute of Mental Health showed that recidivism rates among the youths committed to both institutions dropped 10 percent after the new treatment methods were introduced.

"But behavior modification and transactional analysis won't work for all kids," Breed said. "[What you have to do is] apply the appropriate treatment strategy to the appropriate kid. I'm not saying that everything we're doing in California is working. I'm just saying, don't throw the baby out with the bathwater."

133

The Failure of Institutions

Some administrators agreed that for the most part, institutional programs have not worked. A few, like John Manson of Connecticut and Kenneth Schoen of Minnesota, said that institutional programs could not work because whatever was gained via the programs was lost through the inherently destructive character of prisons. The solution, they said, was to tear down or at least depopulate the institutions to the greatest extent possible.

This has also been the prevailing view among those juvenile administrators who agreed with Martinson and other researchers. "When you take a child out of the community," said Jerry Hissong, then-director of Kentucky's Department for Human Resources, "remove him from the family situation, and ship him hundreds of miles from home, [you can't] expect something magical to happen to him."

"Institutions have traditionally failed to incorporate the kind of reality where the youngster can reintegrate," said Max Brand of Missouri's Division of Youth Services. "By and large, I would say that institutional programs have failed."

A handful of administrators said they agreed with the conclusions of the researchers, but added that institutional programs could work if properly implemented.

"If corrections were given the opportunities and the resources, it could work," said Robert McColley, then acting commissioner of the Maryland Division of Correction. "But most correctional institutions, particularly in Maryland, are dealing with modernistic concepts in obsolete facilities. It's like putting a Cadillac engine in a Model T Ford. Most ectional institutions are seriously overcrowded, so you're doing more warehousing than rehabilitation. Under the system we're now operating, no, rehabilitation is not working."

134

Perhaps the strongest statements of support for the argument that programs have failed have come from conservative prison administrators. Russell Lash, former head of the Indiana and Oklahoma prison systems, contended that "The correctional system has little to do with the resocialization process. We can determine prior to a man's incarceration, with a reasonable degree of accuracy, whether he's going to be a recidivist. It has nothing to do with his imprisonment.

"But that doesn't mean that prisons are not effective. While we cannot demonstrate that prison programs are effective, incarceration itself is effective." Lash said that prison acts as a deterrent and also as "an overt demonstration in our society that the rules have been broken. . . . Prisons tell people there's something wrong in breaking the law. If you tear down the walls, you'll have a lawless society." Lash favors the imprisonment of all felons, if only for a short time.

W. J. Estelle, Jr., director of the Texas Department of Corrections, said that articles like Martinson's have given the taxpayers "an unparalleled opportunity to see how their money is being spent. Out of desperation and frustration, correctional administrators have grasped at just any straw floating in the wind. We've been beset by fads and fashions and fadism to the detriment of the taxpayer's dollar.

"I would suggest that we have gone to the legislature too many times [asking for money for new programs] without any empirical evidence to support our argument. The cruelest hoax of all is that we've gone to our inmates too many times and told them if they would subject themselves to whatever our program is they will no longer return to prison."

Texas, Estelle said, has not "indulged in a lot of sophisticated and costly experimentation. . . . We are not very sophisticated and are seen as rather conservative. But we don't apologize to anyone when we review our recidivism rate compared to that of other states."

Many other administrators, while not in agreement with Estelle about the worth of new programs, have believed that during the last decade corrections has been "hoisted on its own petard," in the words of Harvard criminologist Lloyd Ohlin. "It appeals for funds and resources on the grounds that it can effect some rehabilitation and be an effective preventive against recidivism. Those claims have been exaggerated out of a faith, really, in what they were doing. It's hard for people to really invest their energy if they don't believe in what they're doing."

Said R. Kent Stoneman, director of the Vermont Department of Corrections: "Corrections has been terribly overambitious in setting about as if it was going to cure every individual who came along of some grave malady."

Terrell Don Hutto, head of the Arkansas system, said that rehabilitation has been a "dangerous promise. We cannot guarantee it. We're all going to get ourselves in trouble if we don't stop holding out unreal hopes. The state of the art isn't advanced enough for us to say we're gonna rehabilitate everyone."

"When people say there is no effect to anything we do, I churn inside," said Perry Johnson, head of the Michigan Department of Corrections. "The problem is that we have made claims. We have said the guy is sick and we're the doctor and we're going to cure him. A lot of times we fudged it and people are just sick of hearing excuses so they reach to the opposite extreme."

Community Programs

Even among administrators who have been skeptical of the value of institutional programs, there has remained a faith, or at least a hope, that more success could be found in rehabilitation programs that operate on the community level.

Schoen of Minnesota said that the only goal of institutions should be to "not further debilitate the individual" and to get him out as quickly as possible. "The [main] job of corrections is linking up the individual with the various socializing and healing forces in the community. Community programs in themselves don't rehabilitate. [But] keeping [an offender] in the community gives him a chance to function, so that he can mature in an environment that is health-giving rather than debilitating."

Manson of Connecticut, after stating that he did not think institutional programs have worked, went on to say: "I'm not so sure I'd limit that to institutions. There's nothing that's been done that indicates that community programs work, either." Manson had hopes for the "reintegration model" that Connecticut has been implementing. The principle behind it has been to "just get 'em ready as quick as we can and get 'em out of the institutions," and then provide maximum support through community agencies. "It would be comforting," he added, "to have some empirical data to show that that makes sense."

No adult correctional administrators, even the most liberal, have taken seriously the notion that all offenders could be safely and effectively handled in community programs. Estimates of the number who could be released to community programs, or who should never have been imprisoned at all, have ranged from none to 90 percent. Most responses from administrators were that 30 to 40 percent now incarcerated could be in community programs.

Ed Pogue, who had been warden of the Nevada State Prisons, was one of the few administrators with no faith at all in community programs, at least for those offenders who have been in Nevada prisons. "The community programs I've seen haven't been any more effective [than institutional programs]," he said. "A lot of these people are irrational and irresponsible people who need some external controls. Those who can be placed in community programs are the old-time cons for whom programs don't do any good anyhow." Pogue resigned in July 1976.

Estelle of Texas said that many states have gone overboard in their reliance on community programs, especially probation. "I am personally and professionally opposed to crimes of violence being probated from the bench," he said. "I have reservations whether they should be considered for community programs at all. There are few armed robbers in Texas that are probated from the bench. We as a community have reached an intolerable level of violence in the street."

Fixing Responsibility

Many administrators have resented the implication by their critics that it has been their fault somehow that more offenders have not been rehabilitated.

"I refuse to accept the blanket indictment," said John Moran, director of the Arizona Department of Corrections. "I don't think that, despite the rising crime rate and high recidivism rate, you can lay that dog only at the door of corrections. There are a whole series of overwhelming social and economic factors that contribute to [criminality]. The relatively recent surge of drug abuse [for instance] has created more criminals than anything I can put my finger on."

It is true that institutional programs don't work, said Paul Keve, director of adult corrections in Delaware. "But I don't think that's very surprising. If you take somebody that's been damaged for years and turn him out to the same kind of environment he was in before, I don't think it's very surprising that the therapy doesn't hold."

"One has to consider," said Edward Klecker, corrections director in North Dakota, "that the institution is supposed to be the end-all and correct a whole lifetime of errors, beginning with the family. . . . It's asking a bit much of an institution to completely rehabilitate a person whose history goes back to a long stream of failure."

Said Amos Reed: "If all doctors had to guarantee that every person who came to them had to be permanently cured—never have another cold, never break another bone —you'd put all the physicians out of business. To imply that all people have to have a permanent cure when they are subsequently exposed to all the contingencies of the community, areas over which the institution has no control, is nonsense. . . . [If a physician] is treating someone who has influenza and he goes duck hunting and falls in the icy river, to hold the physician responsible for that man's pneumonia is ridiculous."

Administrators repeatedly point out that there is not necessarily any connection between the quality of an institution, or the quality of its programs, and an offender's ultimate success in the community. "There are a hell of a lot of other factors that go into that recidivism rate," said Gerald Hicks of Michigan's juvenile system. "We don't have employment programs for any of these kids. The kids we're talking about have 20 per cent unemployment. And that's only counting the kids who had a job and lost it. The kids are still being booted out of the educational system and can't get back in. . . . It's a matter of supporting gains that people make. If you take a kid and get him into a nondelinquent thought process and then drop him back on Twelfth Street in Detroit, and you don't do anything to support him, then . . ." He didn't finish the thought.

If an offender who goes through a program does not succeed in the community, the administrators said, it does not necessarily mean that the program is flawed. "We tend to say that the rates of recidivism evaluate the program," said Samuel Sublett of Illinois, "but that's obviously not true."

Howard Leach, then secretary of the New Mexico Department of Corrections, said that "one of the basic problems has been the failure to recognize that skills work in the service of basic attitudes—that simply patching new skills on inmates without touching upon the attitudes out of which he uses these skills will only result in more skilled manipulation in violation of laws. We have ended up with simply a lot of dishonest fenderpounders who have gone through these programs, but their attitudes haven't changed."

How can one change "basic attitudes"? The method in prisons of a hundred years ago was religious instruction. In recent years it has been group therapy. There has been no evidence, according to researchers, that either has had any impact. In fact, Robert Martinson found one study that indicated that a group of offenders who had gone through group therapy did *worse* on parole than a comparable group that hadn't.

Many observers are convinced that it was the failure of traditional kinds of therapy and counseling that led in recent years to the popularity of programs designed to force inmates to change their attitudes; that is, behavior modification. "If people really wanted us to change offenders," said Ed Pogue, "there wouldn't be any controversy over behavior modification and aversive therapy. But they want us to be nice and at the same time rehabilitate people."

A large number of adult administrators said that any effort to force offenders to change their basic attitudes has been futile. "I can't rehabilitate an offender," said Raymond Helgemoe, warden of the New Hampshire State Prison. "He can [only] rehabilitate himself."

R. Kent Stoneman of Vermont said he was only interested in providing programs for inmates who come to "some internal decision point" to change their life styles. "It is a waste of time to scatter-gun psychiatric or social work counseling or education programs [on everyone]. . . . We begin by asking inmates to write their own programs. . . . If a person chooses to say, 'I want to pull [just serve] my time,' we say, 'Okay, pull your time.' "

The strongest statement came from Norman Carlson of the U.S. Bureau of Prisons. "People can change," he said. "Offenders can change. They change because they are motivated to take advantage of opportunities, not because of anything that we do to them or for them. We should get away from the medical model, which is essentially that you diagnose and treat. We can't diagnose and treat offenders, because first of all we don't know what we're diagnosing and second of all, we don't know what works and what doesn't work."

Carlson said that the federal system had completely reversed itself on this issue in the last ten to fifteen years. It was in the federal system that many group-therapy, behavior-modification and similar programs were first tested. Carlson gave this example of a program that was tried and abandoned in the federal system: "We started a program at the Kennedy Youth Center in Morgantown, [West Virginia,] where we labeled inmates and assigned them to housing units based on behavioral categories. We had a questionnaire and a series of observations made by the staff. On the basis of these evaluations, inmates were assigned to one of four behavioral categories. They were scientifically documented by a psychologist. And then we tried to develop some specific treatment modalities for each group. We have given up on the whole damn thing."

Though most administrators, like Carlson, have had little confidence in the ability of specific programs to turn offenders around, this has not meant, they emphasized, that the correctional system has not changed offenders. It may just mean, they felt, that the rehabilitative process is more vague and mysterious than many of the "treaters" are willing to admit.

"It's just very difficult to establish what does and does not change people," said Charles Adams, director of the Division of Corrections in Alaska. "It's too difficult to say that because a man went to group therapy, that's what kept him from getting in trouble again. You have to provide the man with the opportunities to change, but I don't think that you can ever say that this or that program did or did not do it."

"It's a bogus thing to say that because the programs don't have a measurable effect on parole outcome, we should eliminate the programs," said Jiro Enomoto, director of the California Department of Corrections. "I don't think most of the things we do in prison are that concrete, that measurable."

Administrators pointed out that many offenders do not get in trouble again after leaving prison—estimates range from 30 to 60 percent—and they said that institutional experiences must have deterred at least some offenders from crime.

"I'm rather interested in something that no one is responding to on the national level," said the late Elayn Hunt of Louisiana. "How do you explain the *success* rate? I don't see any articles saying that the success rate happens despite the system. No one has documented that. There is a success rate."

"Something good must have been done somewhere," said Moran of Arizona. "The older cons are no longer with us in the percentages they used to be. Maybe something rubbed off on them and they did take advantage of rehabilitation programs and straighten out their lives."

Several administrators expressed the opinion that the most important thing the corrections system can do for an offender is bolster his ego. "I have a deep-seated feeling that a lot of what we are dealing with is the self-image of people," said Hutto of Arkansas, "and that any program that contributes to the enhancement of personal self-image and helps them to think of themselves more as successes than failures helps them to function more effectively."

Ward Murphy, director of the Maine Bureau of Corrections, agreed. "Any program in a correctional institution that gives a person more security or personal esteem or helps him to assume a more acceptable place in the world he is going to live in helps a person to stay out of trouble with the law," she said. Murphy also stated that the single most important element in changing many offenders' attitudes and behavior has been the correctional staff. She shared this view with Bureau of Prisons' Director Carlson.

"A substantial number of inmates don't get back into trouble," Carlson said. "Why? I think the most important aspect of an institution is the interpersonal relationship between an inmate and a staff member. The inmate finds a staff member he can relate to, is polite to him, is courteous, is interested in him. I think that is the most significant single factor in an institutional program. It's not vocational education; it's not psychoanalysis. . . . You talk to [former] inmates and the thing they recall most vividly is the one or two staff members who they really felt were interested in them and encouraged them to try to straighten out."

Some reformers and academic observers have criticized the theory that staff-inmate interaction plays a major role in rehabilitation. They said that the great majority of inmates, especially in large institutions, have very little interaction of any kind with staff members. The people that inmates have come into most contact with, they added, are guards, and the relationship between inmates and guards has more often than not been very formal or even openly hostile. In urban states the possibility of a warm relationship developing between staff and inmates has been even more remote, they said, since most of the inmates are black and most of the staff white.

Some officials support another theory—that has little to do with anything in the criminal justice system—to explain why many offenders do not return to crime. The theory is that many offenders, when they reach a certain age, "mature out" of the correctional system. While criminologists have known about this phenomenon for many years, it has recently become the subject of renewed interest.

Various studies have shown that the maturation process occurs at two points in criminal careers. Recidivism among juveniles remains high until they reach their late teens, when the rate drops sharply—as much as 50 percent. Recidivism among adults also remains high until they reach the age of about thirty-five, when it again drops off sharply.

"One of the greatest tools we have," said Don Erickson, director of the Idaho Bureau of Correction, "is the chronological age. Regardless of what we do, they're going to grow older and reach a maturity. That has a lot of bearing [on whether they continue to get involved in crime]."

Francis Maloney, commissioner of the Connecticut Department of Children and Youth Services, said that when he was a student in college twenty years ago, one of his professors warned him not to place too much faith in programs: "He said if you could hang a youngster on a coat hanger for a couple of years, his maturing will do more than all your programs." Maloney said that experience has borne out his professor's warning.

Robert Martinson said that no study has ever attempted to explain exactly why maturation affects prisoners this way. "I cannot think of a single more important study than an understanding of the delinquency dropout rate, as I like to call it," he said.

The common-sense explanation of the dropout rate for

juveniles, administrators and researchers say, is that delinquents simply tire of the criminal antics that excited them when they were young.

For adults, the process may be more of a burning out than a maturing out. "Crime is, after all, a young man's game," said criminologist Lloyd Ohlin. "Offenders do eventually get tired or feel they can't make it any more."

Ohlin agreed with many adult administrators that "you almost have to wait until the person himself is willing to turn around, then almost anything works, any kind of help and assistance." One must remember, he added, that "lives of crime in many respects have paid off for a lot of these guys. So they've done a little jail time. They've alternately been rich and broke. They haven't been able to lead any kind of settled life, but they've wanted excitement. The life-style has appealed to them. When that no longer seems either feasible or attractive, then they begin to search for some other things. Maybe some prison time is essential to get that to set in. The problem is sorting out those for whom that is the only answer from others who are maybe ready to turn around. We don't do well at predicting each other's behavior."

Chapter 7
The Future for Corrections

We must destroy the prison, root and branch. That will not solve our problem, but it will be a good beginning. . . . Let us substitute something. Almost anything will be an improvement. It cannot be worse. It cannot be more brutal and more useless.

— *Frank Tannenbaum, 1922*

Prisons have few friends; dissatisfaction with them is widespread. They are too frequently the scene of brutality, violence and racial conflict. And insofar as prisons purport to cure criminals of crime, their record has not been encouraging. Nevertheless, prisons have other purposes—to punish, to deter, to banish—which assure their continued survival. — *Norval Morris, 1974*

Despite the noble sentiments and tireless work of Tannenbaum and hundreds of reformers like him over the last fifty years, hardly a stone in the high walls of America's fortress prisons has been dislodged. And if one accepts the arguments of modern "realists" like Morris, it is unlikely that the number of prisons, or prisoners, will soon diminish. In fact, there is every reason to believe that in the next few years, if the crime rate and public fear of crime continue to escalate, there will be more people in prison than ever before.

The exact number of men and women who are banished from free society, and the conditions of their confinement, may depend to a large extent on how successful modern reformers are in altering a criminal-justice system that according to many observers has suffered miserably in the past at the hands of those who would cure it of its ills.

The major critics, both individuals and organizations, who are today actively pressing for prison reform, follow two distinct courses. These two schools of thought might be labeled "abolitionism" and "pragmatism," with Tannenbaum and his successors falling into the first category and Morris and his adherents into the second.

Those in the abolitionist camp tend to favor drastic action —either the total elimination of the prison or a vast depopulation under which only that tiny minority of offenders considered "dangerous" would remain behind bars. These reformers consider most offenders to be victims of a socio-economic system that harshly discriminates against the poor and minorities. They argue that no real justice can exist until society reorders its economic priorities and purges itself of the racism that affects all of America's institutions, especially the criminal-justice system.

Most of the abolitionists would agree with the following statement from *Struggle for Justice*, a 1971 book published by the American Friends Service Committee: "The quest for justice will necessarily be frustrated so long as we fail to recognize that criminal justice is dependent upon, and largely derives from, social justice. The only solution for the problem of class and race bias in the courtroom or by the police or correctional system is the eradication of bias from American life."

The members of this reform group regard themselves as

147

"humanists." As humanists they consider imprisonment, especially in American correctional institutions, to be inimicable to the dignity of man. "Any coercion of another human being goes against our deep respect for every person's dignity," says *Struggle for Justice*. "We believe that all people have the right to autonomy and privacy, to be left alone to find their own way."

While the abolitionists recognize the need for order and rules in society, they believe, in the words of the authors of *Struggle for Justice*, that "if the choice were between prisons as they now are and no prisons at all, we would promptly choose the latter. We are convinced that it would be far better to tear down all jails now than to perpetuate the inhumanity and horror being carried on in society's name behind prison walls. Prisons as they exist are more of a burden and disgrace to our society than they are a protection or a solution to the problem of crime."

The abolitionists outside the corrections system, as most are, are well aware that they have no power to effect their goals, except the power of persuasion. Therefore, most of them are involved on a day-to-day basis in more practical programs aimed at ameliorating conditions within the prisons, helping prisoners to assert their rights and assisting ex-offenders to readjust to the free community. For the kind of massive upheaval that is their principal program, they must rely on allies within the correctional system like Dr. Jerome Miller, the commissioner who closed the juvenile institutions in Massachusetts.

The abolitionists admit that they sometimes sink into despair when after many years of work they look at the correctional system and see that most of the institutions have changed little. On the other hand, some observers give the abolitionists credit for effecting enormous change. They point to the sharp rise in activity by lawyers inside prisons, and to the increasing intervention by federal judges acting on inmate claims of denial of their constitutional rights.

Even more important, the abolitionists take much of the credit for holding the prison population stable throughout the sixties and early seventies despite a huge increase in both the rate of crime and the number of convictions. By exerting pressure on officials to declare a moratorium on new prison construction, and by campaigning to expand the number of offenders diverted to probation and community programs, the reformers may have kept tens of thousands of offenders out of prison cells.

Many of the "pragmatists" profess to hold the same ideals as their more "radical" colleagues in the prison reform movement. Some of them also favor large-scale depopulation. All of them favor the elimination of the American "mega-prison" and its replacement with smaller, more humane institutions.

But they place most of their emphasis not on long-term programs to abolish prisons, and social injustice along with it, but on more short-term, practical solutions to what they term the worst injustices of the present system. Mostly members of the academic community, the pragmatists maintain more amicable ties with government officials and legislators than their more radical colleagues. In fact, many of them have been the recipients of government grants to study the criminal-justice system and its reform. For this reason, the more radical of the abolitionists, who view them as the chief manufacturers of the endless studies and reports that result in no real change, denounce them for seemingly having been co-opted by the government.

In her book *Kind and Usual Punishment,* Jessica Mitford lashes out at the "ever-proliferating ancillary interests that stand to gain from the widespread demand for prison reform. New tentacles of the prison octopus are growing, nourished by immense sums made available through government agencies, universities, private foundations. . . . There is little wonder that architects, researchers, professionals in half a dozen lines of endeavor are standing in line with their hands out. There are fortunes to be made, and professional prestige to be gained, on the correctional trail."

The pragmatists take it for granted, though some have to swallow hard first, that there will always be prisons. Having accepted this, they have begun to re-examine the fundamental precepts underlying the whole system of criminal sanctions, from probation to prison to parole. Even the most casual look at the history of the American criminal-justice system, they point out, reveals that for the last hundred and fifty years its major thrust has been to try to reform, rehabilitate or treat the criminal offender. This is the worst aspect of the system, they now conclude. Not only do these critics assert that we have no evidence that rehabilitation programs work, but they also argue that it would be fundamentally unjust to make an offender's date of release from prison contingent on his progress in those programs even if they did work.

In what amounts to a complete reversal of the traditional reformist position on the purpose of prisons, these pragmatic critics now say that those who commit crimes, especially serious crimes, should be punished, not treated. Furthermore, they state that the punishment should be approximately equal for all those convicted of the same crime. The type and severity of that punishment are matters of dispute. But the pragmatists agree that the worst enemies of any correctional system trying to treat everyone uniformly and justly are the indeterminate sentence and the parole board.

These critics have proposed to do away with both and adopt a flat-sentencing system. The abolitionist group, though often for different reasons, has also endorsed this plan, and together they have exerted heavy pressure on legislatures in a dozen states to adopt flat sentencing. The state of Maine was the first to do so. The idea also got powerful support in February 1976 when U.S. Attorney General Edward Levi called for a sharp curtailment of the sentencing discretion of federal judges and for the abolition of the U.S. Parole Board.

The critics' opposition to the indeterminate sentence and parole stems from the broad conviction that the existing criminal-justice system permits so much discretion to prosecutors, judges, prison administrators and parole boards that in effect, the rule of men has supplanted the rule of law, resulting in tremendous disparity in sentencing and time served.

U.S. District Court Judge Marvin Frankel, in his widely quoted book *Criminal Sentences: Law Without Order*, writes: "The almost wholly unchecked and sweeping powers we give to judges in the fashioning of sentences are terrifying and intolerable for a society that professes devotion to the rule of law. . . . The result . . . is a wild array of sentencing judgments without any semblance of the consistency demanded by the ideal of equal justice."

Leonard Orland, a professor of law at the University of Connecticut, argues in his recent book, *Prisons: Houses of Darkness*, that "the process by which the law sends lawbreakers to prison (sentencing); the processes by which those lawbreakers are confined (imprisonment); and the process by which those same lawbreakers are released (parole) are largely lawless."

The Abolitionists and Their Program

"Every generation of Americans, from the first days of the Republic to our own times, has produced a dedicated coterie of prison and asylum reformers," wrote historian David Rothman two years ago in the *Civil Liberties Review*. "Yet

151

each generation, it seems discovers anew the scandals of incarceration, each sets out to correct them, and each passes on a legacy of failure. The rallying cries of one period echo dismally into the next. . . . We inherit, in essence, a two-hundred-year history of reform without change."

Rothman, a professor at Columbia University, is the author of what is widely considered the seminal work on the origins of the American prison and mental hospital, *The Discovery of the Asylum.* In that book he traces the history of the prison from the opening of the Walnut Street Jail in Philadelphia in 1790 through the post–Civil War period, when the map of the United States was dotted with penitentiaries and reformatories. These institutions were built, he writes, by high-minded reformers who were convinced that the harsh prison regimen would cure the criminal of his deviant proclivities. They believed, as Rothman says in *Civil Liberties Review,* that "in well-ordered, rigid, disciplined and regimented settings, the deviant would learn the rules for right living that he had not acquired in the chaotic, mobile, open and ultimately corrupting community outside. . . . Even as the disparity between rhetoric and reality became apparent to many observers in the late nineteenth century, the notion of incarceration as cure continued. Indeed . . . more than a trace of it is alive today."

What distinguishes the new breed of prison reformers from their predecessors, in Rothman's view, is their total abandonment of the notion that prisons can, or should even try to, rehabilitate. In fact, they have adopted the opposite view: that all prisons, however new, well staffed, or well equipped, are profoundly harmful; that they systematically destroy all of the best instincts of those they imprison; and that they make offenders more likely to commit crimes when they are released than when they were committed. For this reason alone, reformers argue, the prison must ultimately be abolished.

"They're unreformable," says Dr. Miller. "The whole idea of prison reform is a contradiction." Those reformers who continue to fight for improvement of conditions within the prisons will fail like all the rest have failed for a hundred and fifty years, Miller says. "They'll end up with no reforms to speak of and worse institutions. Massive and quick social change is much more effectively and easily done than slow, phased change. Those who have been talking about basic change and have [instead] moved in a classic reform way will find their whole system betrayed."

Unlike Miller, very few of the most outspoken abolitionists have ever sat behind a commissioner's desk. But this is not to say that they are without power. By far the largest and most influential organization in the abolitionist camp is the National Council on Crime and Delinquency (NCCD). NCCD's 110 full-time staff members work at its main office in Hackensack, New Jersey, and its five regional offices around the country. NCCD also operates lay "citizen councils" in many states and a research center at the University of California at Davis. NCCD has done surveys under contract to various state and local correctional agencies and has provided technical assistance.

NCCD was founded as the National Probation Association in 1907, a time when probation for criminal offenders was considered a radical program, since community alternatives to imprisonment were virtually unknown. Throughout its history, NCCD has remained a stalwart defender of community corrections. One of the first organizations to develop formal standards for the operation of adult and juvenile correctional institutions, for probation and parole, and for the operation of halfway houses and other diversion programs, NCCD joined the ranks of the abolitionists in 1973. In a policy statement from its board of directors it declared that no "nondangerous" offender should ever be imprisoned, and narrowly defined "dangerous" offenders as those with records of persistent violence who were also mentally disturbed. Not more than 10 to 20 percent of the offenders then confined could meet this criterion, the statement maintains.

At the same time, NCCD called for a moratorium on the construction of new prisons, saying that any new construction should be part of a comprehensive correctional plan that would provide "noninstitutional alternatives" for the vast majority of offenders. Since then, NCCD has actively opposed—through lawsuits, internal lobbying and public statements—new construction plans all over the country. NCCD Executive Director Milton Rector said that his organization, sometimes in coalition with other groups, had successfully prevented the construction of new institutions in Illinois, Washington State, Washington, D.C., and several other jurisdictions.

Rector said in an interview that in some parts of the country he and his staff have acquired a reputation as "radicals" and "troublemakers." After NCCD announced its opposition to the proposed construction of new prison cells in one state, Rector charged, some of that state's officials were so angry that they went to all of NCCD's funding sources and tried to persuade them to cut off funding. NCCD has received most of its income from community fund-raising efforts, like the United Way, and from corporations and private foundations.

NCCD also said it lost many friends in Washington, D.C., in 1972 when it came out against the U.S. Bureau of Prisons' $500-million building program. NCCD not only opposed the new construction but called for the abolition of the Bureau of Prisons and the transfer of its inmates to state institutions and community programs.

In the March 1976 issue of *Crime & Delinquency*, an NCCD quarterly journal, Rector, who has been with the organization for more than thirty years, writes: "A nation founded on respect for individual liberty acknowledges that a civilized way to deal with crime excludes exile, excludes mutilation, excludes the death penalty. The punishments of exile, mutilation and death have been abolished because they are excessive; imprisonment of an offender who is not violently assaultive—not dangerous—should be abolished for the same reason. . . .

"Short of killing the offender, imprisoning him is the most violent response a government can make to crime. Despite the great cost of imprisonment and the high ratio of staff to inmate population, government has proved itself incapable of reducing violence within its prisons or of protecting those within its prisons from severe physical or psychological damage. Its rehabilitation and vocational training programs, which are supposed to return the prisoner to his home and his community better motivated and better equipped to avoid crime, have demonstrated no capacity to protect the public or to overcome the disabling effects of incarceration. . . ."

The argument that prisons are a "disabling" force, that they do nothing more than turn their inmates into wild beasts, has been a mainstay of the reformist critique since the nineteenth century. But until recently, the reformers' solution to this problem was to advocate the construction of new, more comfortable and therapeutic institutions. This, the abolitionists maintain, has done more to aggravate the problem than solve it. In an interview David Rothenberg of New York's Fortune Society described these new prisons as "pastel fascism."

The Fortune Society is one of the largest ex-offender organizations in the country. Founded by Rothenberg, a former actor, in 1968, it has always maintained that the government could safely release all but about 15 percent of the men and women now in prison. The increase in the prison population, says Rothenberg, means that the politicians and judges are "dumb." "They know that the longer somebody stays in, the less likely they are to function when they come out. Yet they continue to ignore that. It's an exercise in futility. The greatest single cause of crime in this country is the prison system. I've always felt that, and I still do, and the more they're insistent on longer sentences, the more they are assuring us of having alienated, antisocial, angry, violent people.

"We deal with people coming out of prison, and the greatest single thing we have to do here is to undo the prisonization. We have to de-prisonize people, to overcome the elements of the violent subculture [in prison]. People who commit violent acts on the street are committing isolated acts of violence in a culture that's quasi-violent. When they go to prison, violence is almost an acknowledged means of existence. It's reinforced, it's nurtured."

Rothenberg long ago abandoned the notion that there was any possibility of rehabilitation in prisons—long before any studies supported that thesis. He has rejected, however, the contention that community programs cannot rehabilitate. Most of the community programs that have been studied, he says, have been run by "the charlatans and the ripoffs and the corrections people who redefined their own jobs to get a lot of government money. They were programs that were guaranteed not to work."

While people like Rothenberg and Miller have never placed much faith in the viability, or reformability, of institutions, many critics have only recently come to that conclusion. Perhaps the most prominent example is former U.S. Attorney General Ramsey Clark.

Many present-day reformers and academics point to his book *Crime in America,* published in 1970, as one of the best examples of the "classic," or "traditional," approach to prison reform. In that book Clark adopts the "medical model" of corrections, declaring that "most prisoners suffered from some mental disturbance at the time they committed crime." He writes that corrections is the "most neglected" component of the criminal-justice system, even though "corrections is by far the best chance we have to significantly and permanently reduce crime in America," and advocates increased budgets for the state and federal corrections apparatus.

Clark also states that "rehabilitation must be the goal of modern corrections. . . . Rehabilitated, an individual will not have the capacity—cannot bring himself—to injure another or take or destroy property." To achieve rehabilitation, he endorses the indeterminate sentence, arguing that only such a sentence will give offenders the "incentive" they need to participate in programs. "Indeterminate sentencing affords the public the protection of potentially long confinement without the necessity that long sentences be served."

In more recent statements, Clark has said that he has lost faith in the ability of prisons to reform criminals and favors "the elimination of the prison as we now know it." In an interview Clark said that "the big houses can't work and we need to eliminate the notion of reforming them because they can't be reformed. The concept is wrong, the concept of isolated, remote confinement." Clark went on to say that of those confined, "more than eighty percent would pose a smaller future risk to society if not confined."

But Clark has not totally retreated from his former position. He said he was "impatient" with those who declare that rehabilitation programs don't work and that offenders should be imprisoned solely for punishment and for a fixed period of years. "It's really in vogue now to say, 'None of that reform stuff works,' and therefore you shouldn't do anything—that you ought to just eliminate the indeterminate sentence, build prisons and stick people in them for a set period of years and do nothing for them except feed them and give them a chance to brush their teeth every once in a while, and then turn them loose. There's almost a bitterness in that."

Clark explained that he has been suspicious of those who claim that programs don't work, because "I don't think they can really show me a place where we ever gave any single program an adequate opportunity, when you get right down to it. It's been a poor-boy operation from the word go. . . ."

The Pragmatists

Much of the recent prison reform activity in the United States can be traced to the 1971 insurrection at the Attica Correctional Facility in New York.

New York Times columnist Tom Wicker, an eyewitness to the Attica rebellion, wrote a book, *A Time to Die,* about the experience. Despite all the reformist activity, Wicker does not think that Attica has brought about much real change in the prison system.

"I don't see any evidence that there's more public concern," Wicker said in an interview, "and that's what really matters in the long run. And I think that's understandable. It's not defendable, but it's understandable.

"In my judgment . . . year in and year out, fear of crime is the number-one political issue in America. Not crime—fear of crime. And the politicians play on that fear. You take a fellow out in Queens [a borough of New York City] with three locks on his door. He's going to work every day, maybe moonlighting at two jobs, doing the best he can. I just do not expect that fellow to be very sophisticated about his corrections philosophy. He's scared. And what does he want? He wants more people in prison and he wants them kept there longer.

"In the year after Attica, I made a lot of speeches, on the theory that if people understood their self-interest in this

matter, it would make some difference. [I thought] that if
you could go out to that guy in Queens and say, 'Look,
prison costs you too much—twelve thousand dollars a year
to keep them up in Attica—and for nothing. They aren't
really doing any good, because we know the recidivism is so
high, and the chances are good that you're makin' more
criminals up there than you're rehabilitating. . . .' I thought
that if you were to go around and preach that doctrine, and
if enough people did it, that it would make some difference.
But I don't really think it does. Self-interest is a very powerful motivating force, but it's not as powerful as fear. And
people are afraid. And they just want those criminals locked
up."

Though Wicker said he sympathized with the goals of the
abolitionists, he believed that the more realistic course of
action would be to accept the ugly necessity for prisons and
set about trying, first, to make them more humane, and
second, to eliminate the "arbitrariness and unfairness" of
the process by which offenders end up there.

Wicker cited the reforms outlined in Norval Morris' book
The Future of Imprisonment as the model he would adopt.
Many others, including Norman Carlson, director of the
U.S. Bureau of Prisons, have enthusiastically endorsed Morris' proposals. In fact, Carlson intended to design the treatment program for the controversial federal institution at
Butner, North Carolina, around a model prison for the
"repetitively violent" described in the last chapter of Morris' book.

Morris, dean of the University of Chicago Law School,
has—like other pragmatists—rejected the abolitionist argument that a prison must, by its very nature, be a brutal and
uncaring institution. He has also anticipated the accusation
that his attempt at reform, like all others before it, is
doomed to failure. He responds in his book: "The misan-
thropic belief that plans will inevitably be misapplied and

corrupted . . . should not be allowed to interdict all scholarly and administrative efforts at reform. In a sense, the radical utopian position, arguing that it is ingenuous to try to improve prisons, damning all reform efforts, and insisting that we concentrate only on the restructuring of society . . . is the ultimate 'cop-out.' It is an abnegation of responsibility."

Morris, like almost all other reformers, has denounced the current system's attempt to relate an offender's release date to his progress in institutional treatment programs. "The model of medical treatment that underlies the present advocacy of prison training programs is itself flawed. It suffers fundamentally from a belief that psychological change can be coerced." He has proposed that all programs, except work programs, be strictly voluntary.

But unlike almost all of the other enemies of the "rehabilitative model," Morris would not eliminate either the indeterminate sentence or the parole board. Instead, he would narrow the range of sentencing options (e.g., instead of zero-to-ten years, one-to-three years) and have a parole board set a definite date of release only a few weeks after the offender entered an institution. That date, which would be re-evaluated just before a scheduled parole, could be changed only if the offender had failed in a mandatory program of graduated community release, beginning with weekend furloughs and then moving to work- or education-release and eventual residence in a halfway house. Such a plan, Morris has said, would both guarantee the uniformity of punishment that justice demands and "rehabilitate the rehabilitative ideal."

Morris has also proposed that a judge decide whether or not to imprison an offender strictly on the basis of the gravity of his crime rather than on a determination of whether he is "dangerous."

Prison administrators have often been confronted with the abolitionist argument that all but 15 or 20 percent of those in prison could be safely released. Those in urban states have responded that if they released 80 or 85 percent of their inmates, and if they based those releases strictly on the gravity of the offenses, the only offenders remaining in prison would be murderers and rapists. The reformers have replied that not all murderers and rapists are still dangerous, and prisons should be reserved solely for offenders who are.

Morris has attacked the reformers' position, contending that attempts by judges, prison administrators and parole boards to predict dangerousness—that is, that an offender will commit another violent crime when released—have been wildly inaccurate in the past. He cited two studies in California, one involving a group of released adult offenders who had been labeled dangerous, and the other involving a group of released juvenile offenders. The predictions that the offenders would commit new violent crimes were wrong for 85 percent of the first group, and 95 percent of the second. It is thus, Morris has argued, profoundly unjust to hold any offender beyond his normal release date on the grounds that he will be dangerous if released.

Norval Morris was, of course, not the first prison reformer to propose a drastic narrowing of the discretion wielded at every level of the criminal-justice system. In fact, one of the first coherent attacks on the "rehabilitative model" and one of the first proposals for a flat-sentencing system were offered in 1970 in *Struggle for Justice.* The book, while advocating the abolition of prisons, recognized that this is "not a real option." If there must be prisons, it reasons, then prison sentences should be exactly equal for all those convicted of the same crime. And the real reason for the prison sentence should be stated baldly: punishment.

The idea of implementing a flat-sentencing system soon began to be seriously discussed in correctional and sociological literature, even though many correctional administrators denounced it as a throwback to the first half of the nineteenth century—the last time fixed terms of imprisonment were generally imposed in this country.

Perhaps the best-known of the flat-sentencing proposals was unveiled by Dr. David Fogel, executive director of the Illinois Law Enforcement Commission, who made flat sentencing the heart of his "justice model" for corrections. Fogel's plan grouped crimes into five different categories, with each category carrying a fixed term, ranging from two years for minor crimes to twenty-five years for murder. It would permit judges to raise or lower the fixed term by as much as 20 percent if there were mitigating or aggravating circumstances, but the law would specifically spell out those circumstances.

This does not mean, Fogel pointed out, that all offenders would go to prison under his plan. He said that he wanted it written into law that only offenders who presented a "clear and present danger" to the public should be imprisoned. The rest should be fined, conditionally released, placed on probation or diverted to halfway houses or other community programs.

Fogel's plan has been strongly attacked by some abolitionists. Both the John Howard Association, a large Midwestern reform organization, and NCCD have come out against it. Both groups charge that the plan would double the number of people currently in Illinois prisons. One reason, they say, is that offenders guilty of serious crimes who get probation under the present system would automatically go to prison under Fogel's plan.

Fogel contends, on the other hand, that his program would drastically reduce the prison population by vastly expanding the number of community programs available to local courts. "The thrust of our bill is to make the courts exhaust less onerous outcomes [than prison] first," he says. If properly implemented, he maintains, the program would result in the diversion of virtually all property offenders—30

162

to 40 percent of the Illinois prison population—to community programs.

Skeptics worry, however, that state legislatures might drastically alter Fogel's and other flat-sentencing plans, with the result that more, not fewer, people will go to prison. "They'll never get beyond the first step," says Jerome Miller. "We'll have longer and longer and more repressive determinate sentences."

Others have argued, however, that we must take the risk. And the best reason why we must, they say, is that in almost every major prison riot of the last ten years, one of the inmates' principal complaints was sentencing disparities and allegedly unfair treatment by parole boards. With these facts in mind, the Field Foundation in 1971 formed the Committee for the Study of Incarceration. Made up of prominent sociologists and legal scholars, plus a historian (Rothman), a psychiatrist (Willard Gaylin) and a philosopher (Marshall Cohen), the committee issued its final report in 1975 in book form, *Doing Justice: The Choice of Punishments.* The report was written by the head of the committee's staff, Andrew Von Hirsch, a lawyer and professor of criminology at Rutgers University.

The committee's proposals are a delicate compromise between the abolitionist and pragmatist positions. The report disposes of the rehabilitative model in summary fashion. Even when the committee began its work, Von Hirsch says, "the old rationale was literally dead on its feet, and it was a matter of simply giving it a gentle shove." The report proposes to do away with the indeterminate sentence and the parole board, and suggests a schedule of flat sentences ranging in length from one to five years, and covering all crimes except murder.

The rationale behind the committee's new sentencing system is punishment, pure and simple. Why should the criminal offender be punished? Because he "deserves" to be

163

punished, the committee concluded. In fact, the committee chose the phrase "commensurate deserts" as its guiding principle.

Having decided that the criminal deserves to be punished, however, the committee then rejected imprisonment as too severe a punishment for all but the most serious crimes. First offenders, or offenders convicted of nonserious crimes, would receive one of many proposed "lesser punishments," including stiff fines, intensive supervision in a redesigned probation system or periodic imprisonment on evenings or weekends. Those sent to prison would be committed under a formula that weighed both the gravity of their current offense and their prior record.

The report emphasizes again and again that existing maximum sentences for almost all crimes are too harsh. Von Hirsch points out, however, that under the committee's proposal those offenders sent to prison would serve no less actual time than most do now. On the average, inmates in U.S. prisons have been serving from two to five years, depending on the crime. To illustrate the difference between the current system and the committee proposal, Von Hirsch paraphrases a cartoon he once saw in which a judge is saying, "Well, some days you feel bad and you give 'em ten years, and other days you feel good and you give 'em probation. But it all averages out."

The committee's final report was not unanimously accepted; four of the fifteen committee members wrote dissents, which are published as an appendix to *Doing Justice*. One of the dissenters is Herman Schwartz, a university professor and former American Civil Liberties Union attorney. Though Schwartz endorses the committee's proposed sentencing plan, he rejects its reasons for adopting it. "I do not believe that the deserts principle should serve as one of the principal rationales for a system of punishment," he writes. "Can one really say that someone *deserves* [his emphasis] to be punished for breaking the law, when that person may have been hooked on heroin by the time he was a teenager, was confronted with racism and other prejudice, grew up in a broken home amid violence, filth and bruality, was forced to go to substandard schools, and had no honest way to make a decent living?"

Most active prison reformers, both abolitionists and pragmatists, have not made serious claims that their prescriptions for change would significantly reduce crime. They have justified them for the most part on the grounds that they are more fair than the existing system. Von Hirsch says that his committee did not even deal with the issue of reducing crime, since its members were convinced that little could be done to the criminal-justice system that would affect the crime rate one way or the other.

There is an author, however, who does claim that crime can be reduced significantly through the reform of the criminal-justice system—James Q. Wilson. Reform may not be the proper word for the proposals of this pragmatist, since the word has come to mean a reduction in prison populations, and Wilson's proposals, if implemented, would probably mean that many more people would go to prison.

Wilson, professor of government at Harvard University, argues in his book *Thinking About Crime* that government agencies, especially the courts, reacted to the crime wave of the sixties and seventies in a way that was obviously detrimental to their own best interests—that is, by "isolating" or imprisoning a smaller and smaller percentage of those convicted of crimes. Since repeaters commit most serious crimes, he asserts, "the gains from merely incapacitating convicted criminals may be very large," and "may produce very large reductions in crime rates."

Wilson scoffs at the argument that prisons themselves are factories of crime. "It is no defense of this policy of deprisonization," he writes, "to say that criminals, if sent to

165

prison, would on their release merely resume the commission of crimes. Many no doubt would, but the gains to society from crimes not committed while they were in prison would be real and substantial, and if the policy of prison sentences were consistently followed, even with relatively short (one or two years) sentences, the gains would be enduring."

Wilson goes on to contend, though with less confidence, that the certainty of imprisonment for all serious crimes might deter others from yielding to temptation. Most criminals are capable of weighing the costs and benefits of their actions, he reasons, and if the costs are too high, at least some of them will refrain from criminal acts.

Many reformers, whether they are abolitionists or pragmatists, have denounced in the strongest terms proposals like Wilson's, which call for increased incarceration.

The mention of James Q. Wilson threw David Rothenberg into a rage. "James Q. Wilson is an affront to . . . sensibility and problem solving," he said. Rothenberg went on to say that Wilson was quoted so often because he is a "Harvard hardhat, and that makes him good copy."

Jerome Miller noted that the United States already "has more people in prison per capita than any other Western nation. To add to that as the solution is just crazy." Miller and others have observed with satisfaction that such plans would be impossible to implement because there are simply not enough prisons, and no prospect that legislatures will appropriate enough to build them.

Andrew Von Hirsch asserted that "because Wilson spends so much time on these effectiveness arguments, he doesn't worry much about fairness. [He] assumes that the sentence is primarily a crime control device, and that questions of fairness are secondary." Furthermore, "I just don't believe that the new patented methods of lowering the crime rate are going to be much better than the old ones."

The question to ask those who favor the expansion of the prison system, Von Hirsch said, was: Suppose, in pursuit of a significantly lower crime rate, the size of the American prison system were doubled, and then the crime rate didn't go down?

Wilson's critics also have argued that justice can be done, and offenders punished, without prisons. "One can guarantee justice without getting hung up on whether to imprison or not," Miller said. "You can have punishment that does not destroy people. There are ways in which you can have punishment and justice and still have some healing. There are ways in which you can punish your children without harming them. To talk about justice only in terms of prison or nonimprisonment is terribly unimaginative and banal."

Replying to these criticisms, Wilson said in an interview that he was not in favor of all offenders going to prison, as had often been charged. He believed that most first offenders, most offenders convicted of minor and "victimless" crimes, and all juveniles guilty of "status" offenses could be diverted. But, he added, "I am appalled at the number of persons convicted of serious crimes, and who have been convicted a number of [previous] times, to whom nothing happens."

Wilson said that philosophically, he was "not opposed to locking people up." Even if locking people up who committed serious crimes did not reduce the crime rate, he argued, it would be defensible in terms of justice—justice for both the offender and the victim.

Wilson said that he was as shocked as anyone else at the living conditions in some prisons, but added that there was no evidence, as the reformers contend, that harsh conditions have made offenders more likely to commit crimes when they got out.

While Wilson calls for the greater utilization of prisons for some offenders, Dr. Robert Martinson campaigns for the replacement of prisons with a system that would virtually provide one-on-one supervision. Martinson doesn't fall easily into either the pragmatist or abolitionist camp, though the thrust of his program has seemed to put him in the latter group. Martinson's landmark study on rehabilitation programs helped to inspire much of the current controversy over the future of corrections.

Martinson is firmly convinced that any redesign of the correctional system that does not address the issue of reducing crime is irresponsible. "The folks have just had it up to the ears with this street-crime problem," he says. "We are kidding ourselves if we can't cope with that. . . . I don't mean eliminate it. I mean get it under some moderate degree of control so you don't get a twenty percent leap every year."

Martinson agrees with those who say that putting more people in prison is not necessarily the best solution. "In the history of prison reform," he notes, "the most substantial, important thing that has happened is that we've gone from a situation where everybody was in prison a century ago, to a situation where only one third of the convicted offenders are in the cage today—which means that the prison is already profoundly undermined as the basic mode of handling both the dangerous and the nondangerous offender.

"All I'm suggesting," he says, "is that we proceed on that path. Don't build any more prisons. Tear down the ones you have. But you can only do that to the extent that you can replace them with a viable alternative." That alternative, he says, is contained within the existing system of field supervision—probation and parole.

Martinson proposes a complete revamping of the probation and parole systems so that their only function is surveillance. If 80 percent of the inmates in the prisons were released, he reasons, and 80 percent of the prison budgets and a portion of the police budgets were diverted to funding field supervision, there would be enough money to provide almost one-to-one supervision of offenders in the community. With a probation or parole officer literally following him around for much of every day, the potential offender would have little opportunity "to commit that string of thirty-five burglaries. He's going to get caught the second time or the third time."

Such a system, Martinson believes, would provide almost as much restraint on the offender's criminal activity as the prison cell, without overtly harming him. "Prisons are not bad so much because they brutalize. They're bad because they remove a person from the community" and cut off his ties to the normal world. "The search ought to be for a new form of punishment," he says. "I suggest one. I suggest that probation and parole, rather than being a mitigation of punishment, be the punishment."

Martinson adds that reformers should not look for ways to change or redesign the prison, but for new ways to "restrain" the offender while keeping him in the community. "I don't think we've climbed out of the trees and scrabbled up through the mud for the last thousand years to get stuck with a Rube Goldberg device like the prison. It's got to go."

Events, however, are running in the opposite direction. A majority of Americans seem to favor stricter sentencing by the courts, including the increased use of prison terms. The courts have translated that feeling into action, and in many states, the flow of inmates to prison has been unprecedented.

As a result, many of America's prisons for adult male inmates are overwhelmed by their inmate populations. States are turning increasingly to the use of trailers, to rented and converted space, and in the case of at least one jurisdiction, to consideration of a large ship as a makeshift institution.

People have had enough. They want no more streets always too dangerous to walk, no more multiple burglaries

169

on a block, and perhaps most of all, no more fear.

The certainty of punishment, the fixed sentence with no parole and other get-tough measures are now very appealing, although not to everyone. Some view this movement with fear of their own—fear that it might lead to some sort of repression. Chief Judge David Bazelon of the United States Court of Appeals for the District of Columbia said in a speech: "Our last best hope is to seek out the cause of the criminal act. . . . The path of total reliance on punishment is a superhighway leading to a cowpath." He called proposals for fixed sentences "first steps in a thousand mile journey" toward repression.

It seems certain that the future of corrections, like its past, will be tumultuous.

Index

Index

Index

Index

About the Editor

RICHARD KWARTLER is the editor and publisher of *Corrections Magazine*. A graduate of City College of New York and the Columbia Graduate School of Journalism, he has been an education writer for the Cleveland *Plain Dealer* and a reporter for *Newsday*. He served as Deputy Director of Public Affairs for the New York City Human Resources Administration, as the administrator of a minority training program at the Columbia School of Journalism, and as a consultant on criminal-justice issues for the Ford Foundation before becoming the editor in chief of *Corrections Magazine* in 1974.

Corrections Magazine is the first American publication devoted exclusively to original reporting on prison systems in all fifty states. Published by the nonprofit Correctional Information Service, Inc., its principal funding has come from the Ford Foundation.